The
Intuitive
Body

The Intuitive Body

Aikido as a Clairsentient Practice

Wendy Palmer

North Atlantic Books
Berkeley, California

The Intuitive Body: Aikido as a Clairsentient Practice

Published by
North Atlantic Books
P.O. Box 12327
Berkeley, California 94712

Cover art: Vajrayogini, Buddhist female embodiment of wisdom. *Thangka* in the Karma gadri Eastern Tibetan style, painted by Tamam Kahn.
Cover and book design by Paula Morrison
Typeset by Catherine Campaigne

Printed in the United States of America by Malloy Lithographing

The Intuitive Body: Aikido as a Clairsentient Practice is sponsored by the Society for the Study of Native Arts and Sciences, a nonprofit educational corporation whose goals are to develop an educational and crosscultural perspective linking various scientific, social, and artistic fields; to nurture a holistic view of arts, sciences, humanities, and healing; and to publish and distribute literature on the relationship of mind, body, and nature.

Library of Congress Cataloging-in-Publication Data
Palmer, Wendy.
    The intuitive body : aikido as a clairsentient practice / by Wendy Palmer.
        p. cm.
    ISBN 1-55643-171-6
    1. Aikido—Psychological aspects.   I. Title
GV1114.35.P35   1994
796.8'154—dc20   94-6799
                                                                              CIP

2   3   4   5   6   7   8   9 / 98   97   96   95

This book is dedicated to my children,
Tiphani and Django,
who have inspired me to become a better person.

Contents

Acknowledgments XI

Foreword by George Leonard XIII

Introduction I

Embodying a Dream I

Looking at the Foundations of My Perceptions 4

The Influence of Aikido Traditions in My Life 7

How the Videotape Supplements Work 10

How This Book Works 10

Part I. The Body—Establishing Our Ground

Chapter 1. Coming to the Path 15

A Reference Point and a Technique 16

Into the Present 17

Coming Into Sensation 18

Knowing the River 19

Chapter 2. The Elements of Basic Practice 21

*A Centering Triad: Three Parts
of Attentional Concentration* 23

Utilizing Our Breath 23

Balancing Our Energy Field 24

Feeling Gravity 25

Practicing the Technique 26

Personalizing Basic Practice 26

Practicing and Accepting the Mystery 28

Chapter 3. Adding a Quality 31

   Why a Quality? 32

   Identifying a Quality 33

   Using the Body as the Teacher 34

   A Centerpiece for Practice 34

Chaper 4. Energy and Stability 37

   Energy Follows Attention 38

   Embellishing Our Center Practice 39

   A Spiral-Breath Meditation 40

   Take Your Time 41

Chapter 5. Learning 45

   Approaches to Learning 46

   Interest versus Fear 46

   The Grinch and the "Yes . . . . And, . . ." Technique 48

   Practice and Training 49

   Mistakes 50

   Filling in a Hole 51

Part II. The Mind—Shaping Our Concepts

Chapter 6. The Spirit of Inquiry 55

   The Habit of Interest 55

   The Fine Art of Questioning 56

   A Buoyant State of Curiosity 58

   The Don't-Know Mind 59

Chapter 7. Not-Knowing 61

   A Journey into Emptiness 62

   Timing 63

   Mystery 64

   Strength of Spirit 65

Chapter 8. Intuition 67

Working from a Stable Base 68

Not-Knowing: The Doorway 69

Creating Manageable Pieces for the Process 70

Interpreting 71

Nonverbal Communication 73

Part III. Wisdom Arising—Ways Our Soma is Organized

Chapter 9. The Energetic Field 79

*Shaping Our Field:
Triangle, Square, and Circle* 82

Practicing Being Both Positive and Receptive 84

Chapter 10. Attentional States 87

Dropped Attention 87

Open Attention 89

Ellipted Attention 91

Blended Attention 94

Training Attentional States 95

Chapter 11. Splits 97

Basic Splits in the Body 99

Disembodiment 99

The Observer 100

Three Centers: Head, Heart and Hara 102

Techniques Toward Unification: Healing the Split 103

Override 104

How Do I Know When I Am Unified? 104

Part IV. Embodied Action

Chapter 12. *Irimi* 107

The Spirit of Irimi 107

Facing Our Fear III

Evolving by Manageable Percentages 113

Counterphobia 114

The Irimi *of Questioning* 115

Chapter 13. Different Approaches 119

The Masculine—The Motivating Force 119

The Feminine and Non-Action 123

Balance: Integrating Masculine and Feminine 124

The Magical Turnaround 126

Discovering Aspects of Our Being 127

Chapter 14. The Path Never Ends 131

The Dance of Clarity and Obscurity 134

Our Human Prerogative 136

Part V. Practice Guides

Utilizing Your Breath 141

Balancing Your Energy Field 143

Feeling Gravity 143

Evoking and Choosing a Quality 144

Basic Practice 145

Spiral-Breath Meditation 146

"Yes.... And, ..." Technique 148

Positive/Receptive 149

Dropped Attention 149

Open Attention 151

Metta Meditation 152

Acknowledgments

I would like to express my deepest appreciation to all of those who have helped make this book possible:

George Leonard and Richard Heckler, my partners at Tamalpais Aikido, for more than twenty years of unconditional love and support for developing myself and this work.

Helen Palmer for the power of her belief and confidence in me and this work. I find myself rising to meet the challenge of what she believes I can do.

All of my aikido teachers who have given me the art of aikido, the foundation of this work. And especially: Mitsugi Saotome, Hiroshi Ikeda, Robert Nadeau, and Frank Doran.

Pamela Ricard for her friendship, humor, encouragement, support, and untiring ablility to decipher my hieroglyphics.

Mimi Pulich for jumpstarting and driving the first and critical phase of the editing process.

Ellen Mossman and Vivian Ramsted for their time and energy in keeping the momentum during my early, unsure, and resistant period.

Lindy Hough who, more than four years ago, asked me when was I going to write this book.

Ammon Kahn for his technical agility in translating graphics and drawings from paper to disk.

This book is also inspired by Chögyam Trungpa and influenced by his teachings.

Yet of all the people who have contributed to this book, it is the students, who have come to the classes over the past twelve years, who have provided the inspiration to keep this practice alive and evolving. It is their love and frustration, sadness and joy that have moved me to deepen my understanding of relationships and the energy that orchestrates the way we behave. I hope all of these adventuresome people know they are the intrinsic elements of this book.

I am so grateful to Joan Marie Passalacqua and the karma that brought her to become the final editor. I secretly wanted her to work on this book all along because I have always felt that she really understands this work.

Steve and Susan Harper have also touched and shaped this work. They have generously shared the beauty and power of their way of connecting with life and meeting its problems.

Thank you Phillip Moffitt for your perspective, Tracy Thompson for your spirit, and Michael Aragon for your heart.

And, Tiphani and Django for being who you are and giving me your love.

Foreword

For Wendy Palmer, the martial arts mat is a laboratory of the human spirit, a place less for demonstrating perfect, invulnerable technique than for exploring the mysteries of imperfection, the uses of vulnerability. Her particular art, aikido, gives her all a scientist could desire: plenty of people to work with, an art of practically infinite possibilities within the constraints of an elegant form, and a practice that can vary in intensity from very light to very heavy—potentially a pressure cooker within which little remains unrevealed.

Wendy and I have been practicing aikido together since 1971. We have given many workshops and demonstrations together. In 1976, with Richard Heckler as a third partner, we opened a dojo, Aikido of Tamalpais, a school that has served more aikidoists than we can remember. Still, for me, nothing can quite compare with attending one of her classes as a student.

I'm sitting on the edge of the mat in *seiza*, the Japanese meditation position, already smiling in anticipation, feeling fairly certain that, whatever else, I'll be surprised more than once this evening. Wendy walks onto the mat. She is wearing a white *gi* and blue *hakama*, the floor-length divided skirt of the medieval samurai. At five-five and 120 pounds, with slim wrists and ankles, she might seem delicate, even fragile, except for an unmistakeable presence in the way she moves. She leads us in a bow of respect to the picture of Morihei Ueshiba, the founder of the art, and the class begins.

From the start, it's clear that Wendy is willing—maybe eager is the right word—to take risks the typical martial art teacher would work hard to avoid. A certain technique begs for a skilled attacker to respond with the grace and ease associated with this art. Wendy picks a beginner to work with. A certain technique is particularly difficult to pull off if the attacker towers over the defender. Wendy chooses the tallest man in the class. Another technique pits the raw power of the attacker against the relaxed use of *ki* on the part of the defender. Wendy turns unerringly to a muscular six-footer, a man who does 500 push-ups a day. Sometimes she muffs a throw, an occasion for embarrassment or revenge for many teachers, especially those unsure of themselves. For Wendy, a muff is the occasion for learning. What does this teach me—and all the students—about imbalance or aggressiveness or an inability to stay in the moment?

Wendy loves to work with beginners, to perform a simple technique very slowly. This exquisite pace provides her a microscope of high magnification and fine resolution. She sees detail, texture, the subtle connecting tissue that holds the technique together, all of which might be invisible during a fast throw by an advanced student. She asks a karate-trained aikidoist to stand in front of her and punch at her belly. An experiment: How long, how many split seconds, can she stand there in the open, present-tense, vulnerable state she calls "not-knowing" before making her move? Can she then make the move and control the attacker with a feeling of love rather than aggressiveness?

As the students practice, Wendy moves quietly around the mat, seeing what is generally unseen: the tiny, incremental movements, the unformed emptiness from which each movement emerges, a secret thought revealed in a momentary loss of balance, the clinging web of confusion that connects a childhood trauma to a clumsy, unfeeling throw. She teaches by phrase and example. She pursues significant learning through the angle of a wrist, the inertia of a blow. She is at home in her laboratory, knowing only that the class period isn't long enough, life itself isn't long enough, for the learning she so passionately desires and pursues.

Now this scientist of the spirit has distilled her learning to date in a strikingly original book. *The Intuitive Body* is clearly Taoist in overall tone, a modern Western statement of the 2,600-year-old Chinese philosophy that has inspired Zen and all the "inner" martial arts, a teaching that sees life not as a series of goals to be achieved but as a path to be walked for its own sake, that warns ambitious rulers to govern a large kingdom as they would cook a small fish. But in its particulars, this book is all Wendy, a remarkably successful translation of her unique verbal-physical teaching to the printed page.

The Intuitive Body is by no means designed just for martial artists but rather for all those who want to rediscover, in her words, "a part of ourselves that is wise, kind, and capable of clear and powerful embodied action." In this quest, an aware body is the royal road to the intuitive state. The physical center of the body is "the part of us that remembers we belong to the universe." Since energy follows attention, much of this book is devoted to paying attention to various bodily parts and states. Wendy often teaches by example, even in the written word. In many cases, rather than telling the reader what to do, she simply tells what she does and how she does it, leaving it up to the reader, in true Taoistic fashion, whether or not to follow suit.

The Intuitive Body is a book to be read slowly, to be read again and again. In it you will meet a gifted teacher and discover the essence of a unique teaching. Don't expect to be transformed overnight, for instant transformation is an illusion. To produce long-term change, even the most stunning moment of illumination must have been preceded by or be followed by a long and diligent journey on the path of practice. Here is an eloquent and delightful invitation to step on the path.

George Leonard
January 1994
Mill Valley, California

Introduction

*Out of nowhere a horse
brought us here where we taste love
until we don't exist again. This taste
is the wine we always mention.*

Rumi

Embodying a Dream

When I was a young girl I loved to ride horses. I dreamed of galloping as fast as the wind astride a strong stallion with a long flowing mane. One day that dream came true.

My friend Lynnie and I had watched as one of her father's thoroughbred stallions, appropriately named Bridlefree, was being led "fresh off the track," to a corral with a chain over his nose while he fought and reared, his nostrils flaring red inside. After they put Bridlefree in the corral, the men warned us never to go near him; he was "very dangerous," they said. As soon as they left, Lynnie and I went to Bridlefree, bringing him sugar, carrots, and lots of love and adoration. We would often sneak into the forbidden corral, slide onto Bridlefree's back and marvel about how beautiful, strong, and muscled he felt compared to the mares and geldings that we were accustomed to riding.

One day, I do not know why, we went for the dream. Lynnie jumped on a trusted gelding, bareback with a simple bridle. I put only a lead rope on Bridlefree's halter and once again slid onto his back. We opened the gate to the corral. Lynnie and the gelding began to gallop across a field toward a tree-covered lane. Bridlefree sensed the play and took off, his thoroughbred heart and untamed spirit leaping across the field. We were free!

As we raced toward the lane, I twisted Bridlefree's long mane around my hands. I wanted to stay with him no matter what happened. I was living a dream and determined to live it to the fullest. When we entered the lane, I had to lean way over, sometimes ducking my head below my hands to keep the tree branches from knocking me off. Bridlefree interpreted my position as encouragement and I felt him surge a little more, his muscles driving even harder. I could hear his breath and his hooves rhythmically pounding the earth. When I looked down at the ground moving by so fast, my head swam. I closed my eyes, tightened my grip on his mane, and pressed my body into his as much as I could. I remember trying to feel my way into him. I wanted to become one with him.

The end of the lane was coming up with a sharp right turn that led into a short narrow field. Before that moment, I would have considered it impossible to take the turn at the speed that we were going. Now it seemed that anything was possible. I shifted my weight, moving my head to the right side of his neck. His body responded slightly, and for me it was as if I had whispered in his ear and he had understood me. Bridlefree slipped a little in the turn, but we made it out into the open, grassy field. He slowed himself as he circled and stopped to graze in the lush, green pasture. My body was trembling as I unwound Bridlefree's mane from around my hand. His flanks were heaving and his coat glistened in the sun as he nuzzled the earth and nibbled the succulent grass. I had embodied a dream. I sensed anything was possible.

Sixteen years later I saw aikido for the first time. It was as if a crack in the cosmos opened and a whiff of something forgotten yet familiar passed through me. That whiff was the memory of joining with a power, physically much stronger than me, while being open and receptive to my intentions. It was the feeling of flight, of giving myself with the innocence of total love and admiration. Beauty, grace, power, surrender, all of these stirred my desire to embody the dream again. Having dreams and fantasies is great, embodying them is even greater.

Growing up had seemed to be a journey into fear. When I was young, getting hurt meant little while I was actively pursuing the dream. As I got older, the dream began to fade, and protecting myself—not getting hurt—became the major task. I used my mind to understand things, instead of my body to experience them. At the age of twenty-four, I had read many things about physics and existentialism. I knew and loved the *Tao Te Ching,* but my cells had forgotten that they once hungered after flight, grace, beauty, power, and surrender.

Then, as I saw the movements of aikido, I felt a deep sense of coming home—a returning—like waking up and remembering the part of myself that hungers for the experience of essential contact. The Buddhists call it *tantra,* the part that knows real satisfaction from entering the energetic vortex of universal life and breath rather than standing back and observing.

My heart filled with romantic inspiration and I began aikido training. The vast chasm between what I saw and sensed and what I could do was not entirely surprising, but was nonetheless extremely painful to experience. It was hard to bear the fact that all of the discomfort, both emotional and physical, was brought on by myself. I desperately wanted some part, however small, to belong to my partners. It really felt as if the discomfort was caused by something they were doing to me. I could not be doing all this to myself, could I?

Not until a few years later could I appreciate, in a cognitive way, what a powerful step it is to realize, at the level of physical sensation, that we do orchestrate the situations of our discomfort. The other person is not doing it to us. Once we acknowledge this, we can begin the aikido process of *irimi:* moving into the situation, embracing life, and developing deeper contact with our center.

Our center is the part of us that remembers we belong to the universe, the part that feels no need to protect itself since it is not in opposition. For me, center is fed by desire, passion, and curiosity for the experience of essential contact. The trick is to allow my desire to be stronger than my fear. My aggression, which stems from my fear, pushes back my desire and makes me want to protect myself. To keep from being controlled by my fear, I yearn for the center, the way a lover yearns for the embrace of the beloved, the way a young girl might yearn to gallop bareback astride a great stallion.

Looking at the Foundations of My Perceptions

What is it that allows a young girl's perception of a stallion to be that of beauty, graceful power, and love, while a grown man might see the same stallion as dangerous and mean? Assuming that there is truth in both perceptions, why do some people choose one view and some another? Is it possible that we are completely alone and intrinsically connected at the same time? If so, can we find the right tension between these two extremes? Just as a string in a musical instrument is stretched to exactly the right tension to create the proper harmonic sound, perhaps we can learn to balance the tension between the paradoxes of life. The first step is to examine the elements of aloneness and belonging. By looking at our beginnings, our birth and early childhood, we can see some of the factors that have influenced our perceptions of life.

In my case, I was cared for by my mother and many different nurses. My mother had Multiple Sclerosis and was on crutches from the time I was two years old. She was in a wheelchair by the time I was four. I have no real memories of my mother before the wheelchair. By the time I was eight years old, she was losing her ability to talk and the use of her hands. When I was eleven, my mother could no longer speak and needed to be fed and turned in her bed. She lived until I was twenty-one, and she died at the age of forty-nine.

I had a close psychic bond with my mother. I would feed her, fix her hair, clip her nails, and turn her over—a major task, to be done slowly because of the painful spasms the turning could elicit. I was her interpreter and the role stimulated my intuition. She would make a sound or roll her eyes and I would say, "She wants a drink," or, "She needs to be turned." I knew that my ability to understand my mother made the people around us, my father and the nurses, uncomfortable. They were uneasy with the fact that I could read her so easily, but they were also relieved that they did not have to struggle to figure out what she wanted. The result was that my intuition was never suppressed, the way it is in most children. My intuition was needed too badly to be dampened. They were willing to tolerate the discomfort of a child seeing through them because it made it easier for all of us to cope with this difficult situation.

It was during this period, from the age of five, that I was a fanatic horseback rider. The physical love bond which I could never have with my mother because of her illness was replaced by the bond with my horse, Angie. When things got particularly difficult at home, I would run away to the stable and sleep in the stall with Angie. I had the same nonverbal communication with my horse as with my mother, only Angie was softer and cuddlier, and the situation seemed altogether more forgiving. I felt that I belonged with my horse. The result was that I developed the ability to love and to have emotional connections with animals but not with people.

My perception of people was an area of betrayal and confusion. Why had God betrayed me and made my mother ill? What did she do? What was the matter with people that they could not read each other? Why could they not tell what the other person was thinking and feeling? And finally, why did adults say one thing when they were thinking and feeling another? Why did they not tell the truth? The whole thing seemed dark and alienating to me. My respite was with horses. I found horses to be straightforward, affectionate, and honest. While I had a feeling of belonging with horses, I always felt separate from people, except my mother for whom I was the care-taker. But that was dark too, because somehow I felt responsible, that I should be able to fix this situation, that in some way my mother's not getting better was my fault.

I understand that it is quite common for children to feel respon-sible for the problems and illnesses in their family. In my case, I did not feel so much responsible as the cause of her illness, instead I felt that I should be able to heal her. Somewhere deep down inside, I knew that I was capable of healing her if only I could find the key.

My search for the way to heal my mother led me to Buddhism

and Christian Science which, in retrospect, I find quite similar. Although I learned a lot about perceptions of mind, self, and the material world, my mother continued to suffer and my alienation and bitterness continued to grow. I only felt connected through my experience with horses. I felt as though I saw through and understood people, but most of their actions seemed disconnected. I felt as if I did not belong. I felt that I had failed in my role as caretaker with my mother because I had not succeeded in healing her.

I represented the mythology of Christian beliefs—that of having been cast out of the garden. I thought that if I grew up, learned more, had more power, that I might find the way back. I thought that being older might help, then being married might be the answer, and finally I tried having children. I was always trying to find the relationship that would restore my trust; that would make me feel that I was loved; that would give me the sense that I belonged. What I did not realize was that the relationship that I was searching for out there was inside me all the time. As O Sensei (Morihei Ueshiba, the founder of aikido) said, "The attacker is not out there but within." I believe that the converse is true too, that the lover is not out there but within.

How can we begin to feel love for ourselves? How can we develop a relationship with ourselves that will sustain us when life becomes difficult? Perhaps this is why we are so drawn to work on ourselves. Self-help books abound. Classes, seminars, and workshops thrive. New and traditional styles of personal development draw seekers from all walks of life.

For previous generations, there were often clear social systems that provided guidelines on how to be a man or woman. Authority figures such as parents, police, or clergy represented wisdom or knowing. Many of these systems seemed to break down completely in the 1960s. Authority of church, state, and family was challenged and questioned. The feminist movement destabilized the more traditional roles of men and women, intensifying questions of autonomy, power, and relationship. Western culture entered an identity crisis. Everywhere people seemed to be asking, "Who are we? What is right?" Desegregation, democracy, and student protest movements all flared, sending streams of light, illuminating social inadequacies, social reforms, and new possibilities. Many turned to drugs for escape and new experiences, hoping to glean fresh insights.

As the smoke began to clear in the 1970s, the promises of Utopian existence, where all people could be free, equal, and by implication, happy, had not materialized. We had read the books, had incredible experiences and insights, and yet the most basic element of fulfillment—happiness—still eluded us. After all of the fireworks and the reforms and changes, we still were not happy. And so, we became seekers, travelers on our various paths.

We become seekers because we are hurting or suffering in some way. We think that if we find the right teacher or form or insight our suffering will end and we will be happy. Finding a teacher or a form in and of themselves will not make us happy. This is only the beginning of a process of integration, of deepening and unifying ourselves.

The Influence of Aikido Traditions in My Life

For twenty-three years, my primary path has been aikido, a Japanese martial art and meditation. For me, the most compelling aspect of aikido is intuition, the wisdom that comes from within. Experiencing this wisdom from within has developed trust in my ability to operate skillfully in our fast and complex culture.

Aikido was developed by Morihei Ueshiba, who is usually referred to as O Sensei, which means "great teacher." Aikido is a modern martial art, having its official beginning in the 1930s. O Sensei died in 1969. Most of my teachers studied directly with him. O Sensei's influence as a man and inspired teacher is felt strongly in aikido today. He was a remarkable man, a gifted martial artist whose life was dedicated to *Budo*, the essence of life and universal truth. His devotion to the idea of universal peace and love led him to create a unique martial art which holds as its ideal the intent to love and protect all beings, even those who attack with intent to harm. This is a radical departure from the idea of martial art as self-defense or defending ourselves. The name aikido itself represents the philosophy and intention of the art.

> *ai* means "joining" or "harmony" and has the same sound as the Japanese word for love
> *ki* means "energy" or "life force"
> *do* means "way," and is derived from the Chinese word *tao*.

Do is beautifully described by Donn Draeger in his book, *Classical Budo:*

> The *do* or way rests on a spiritual foundation that is expressed and lived through training in a prescribed manner directed toward an ideal of human behavior, which, in turn, elevates the individual and thus the society in which he lives. All *do* forms aim to remove traditional prejudices from human relationships.... Because the *do* forms train man to be "more human," they are considered to be the true path of humanity; an application of living knowledge that is manifested in acts of *assistance* [italics mine] to other human beings.

Since aikido is a martial art, it deals with physical attacks, and, therefore, provides a perfect laboratory to study our fear and aggression. It was my desire to study and understand my fear and aggression in more detail that inspired me to begin the work that is the basis of this book. I began to find ways to develop conscious embodiment and study relationships—boundaries and intuition. In the conscious embodiment classes, we slow down exchanges that take one or two seconds in aikido and spend one or two hours looking at the patterns that arise within these tiny moments. I have been able to see and work with some deep-rooted, fear reactions that surface in relationships. These reactions form our boundaries or sense of self. Our intuition, which is our most valuable asset in our urge toward unity, cannot be accessed if we are reactive. If we can become stable and get our boundaries squared away, then we will be able to recognize and use our intuition.

Buddhist meditation has played an important part in the development of this work. The practice of sitting down or standing still for a particular amount of time provides us with a form in which we can observe our mental patterns. During my first ten-day, silent meditation retreat, I awakened to the harsh reality that, even without any outside influence, my mind has continuous patterns of fear and aggression, hope, and desire.

One of my teachers, a Tibetan lama named Chögyam Trungpa, has been a major influence in my life and my work. His command of both language and space and his fierce loyalty to the bare truth have helped me begin to accept and acknowledge my dark side—self-loathing, hatred, fear, and guilt. His initial teaching was and still is most powerful. The teaching is: "Give up hope completely—accept what is totally." This teaching gave me a place to begin. Time and time again, I must remind myself of this principle. Ironically, there is an experience of hope in giving up hope. This book is my attempt to provide some inkling of the circular movement of giving up hope and accepting what is.

Irregardless of the particular form we use, it is essential to have a path or way of training. We need to be committed to the long term, years of physical and mental discipline. This commitment includes a meditation practice. Meditation involves sitting or standing up straight, being still, and dealing with discomfort for a certain amount of time every day. The idea is to find a form that prevents self-deception with some kind of built-in feedback mechanism such as the posture in sitting or standing meditation. In aikido and the intuition classes, we use our interactions with our training partner as a means of feedback.

Each person must find his or her own unique and individual path. It is like handwriting—it is distinctly ours, yet it must be legible so it can be read. We must choose practices that are "do-able" and work in our lives as they are. Whatever the path, it will continue to evolve and change just as we continue to evolve and change and allow ourselves to be influenced by our life experiences.

I have been touched and influenced by many teachers from many paths. Much of this experience and learning is brought together in this book. My intent in writing this book is to encourage you to develop the discipline to begin or continue your commitment to your path.

How the Videotape Supplements the Work

The goal of conscious embodiment is to provide support and assistance to those traveling on a path which leads to happiness and fulfillment. I believe the more we know ourselves and support our own growth, the more we can serve others.

Throughout my years of teaching, it was often suggested that I make a video or write a book so that the principles of conscious embodiment and basic practice would reach more people. Gene Thomas, a film and video producer who was taking the class in the Fall of 1990, offered to produce a video about conscious embodiment. By the Spring of 1991, all the right elements had come together and some of the students were willing to be taped as they practiced conscious embodiment techniques—the video, *The Intuitive Body,* was created.

Of the techniques presented in this book, *The Intuitive Body* videotape includes discussion and demonstration of basic practice, attentional states, positive and receptive interactions, and learning. At the end of *The Intuitive Body* videotape is a 15-minute training session which can be used for daily practice. For some people the class experience is overwhelming and using the video to practice allows them to be more present with their situation. I made the tape as an aid for those who have taken the classes and as a source of information for those who are curious about conscious embodiment.

How This Book Works

In this book I am presenting my approach to rediscovering the part of ourselves that is wise, kind, and capable of clear and powerful embodied action. This way of being arises out of what I call the "intuitive state," a spontaneous, intelligent, and creative aspect of ourselves which has not been distorted by our fear and confusion. Intuition usually arises in a nonlinear fashion. In our Western culture, the habit of sequential thought has been given a superior role in respect to the way life is viewed. In my opinion, based on living in this culture and experiencing the result of this priority, it does not work. It has not made us happy. There are millions of years of evolution in our cells. A deep store of wisdom lies within and we must look within to access it. We can use our discomfort and dissatisfaction with life to investigate other possibilities or ways of living. We can invite our intuition, our wise knowing, to govern or lead our choices toward a full embrace of life.

The first part of this book deals with becoming grounded in our bodies. Without a firm root system or foundation, intuitive perceptions cannot be focused into embodied action. The second section discusses mental perception and working with the movement and power of our thoughts. This paves the way for us to find how to create a spacious environment from which the wisdom of our intuition can arise, as discussed in the third section. The fourth part addresses the nature of embodied action: *irimi,* entering fully into life situations, and how to work with our perceptions during the many activities and pressures of life. The practice guides at the end of the book are provided as outlines for quick reference to the techniques described in the previous sections.

It is my hope that you will feel free to take these ideas and make them your own by adjusting them to suit your inner needs. The techniques can be used as they are or changed and integrated into your already existing practice. Each of us is a unique individual. When we are sensitive to our own personal experiences, we lend compassion and support to ourselves by being creative. If we can live in a way that promotes a little more kindness and a little less greed, we will have served ourselves and our planet beautifully.

Part I

The Body— Establishing Our Ground

Chapter One

Coming to the Path

It really boils down to this: that all life is interrelated. We are all caught in an inescapable network of mutuality, tied to a single garment of destiny. Whatever affects one directly, affects all indirectly.

Martin Luther King, Jr.

Walking our own true path is finding our way toward wholeness: the unity of body, mind, spirit, and the everything of the universe. Conscious embodiment assists us in being present with the many experiences of our journey through life. Being more present in our bodies also allows our spirit to more fully inhabit our being. Following and exploring our true path allows us to grow and learn in the physical, mental, emotional and spiritual realms. As we come more fully into our bodies, we are able to know and manifest our true purpose in life.

There are people who have always felt called by some kind of spiritual vision or experience, even from the time they were very young. There are others who are drawn through suffering and difficulty to look beyond the material world of images and things. Often a personal catastrophe will suddenly push a person toward his or her path. In one form or another, impoverishment—feelings of not having enough of something, whether it is love, space, trust, courage, softness, strength, or some other desired quality—often brings people to their path. As an Indian teacher once said, "It doesn't matter why they come, just that they come."

The first step is to look at what is, to make a truthful appraisal of the situations and personal chemistry that created the patterns that lock us into narrow, repetitive modes of behavior. We need some ground or stability in order to take an honest look at ourselves. There is a lot of energy in the raw honest truth. Sometimes we can only look at a little at a time. This means that we need to have a way to rest or go neutral when we become overwhelmed so we can avoid casting blame in regards to our truth. Grounding and centering can help us to tolerate and accept who we are. We want to be able to acknowledge our strengths and our weaknesses.

Some of us orient around a pessimistic, alienated view of life— thinking of life as a struggle or waiting for the proverbial ax to fall. We may habitually wallow around in our emotional feelings. Many of us are so used to feeling alone, lonely, or stuck, that when things go well we become nervous or suspicious. On the other hand, some of us are dedicated optimists who tend to rise above emotional feel- ings. We go merrily along until we fall off a cliff, and then feel shocked and amazed that such a thing could have happened. Some of us use another approach, busying ourselves so we can stay ahead of our feelings. We desire transformation. We want to make everything bet- ter—no pain or suffering. I call this the Pollyanna approach.

Yet another approach takes the "middle way" of Lao Tzu, which is a path of balance, including both the dark and light aspects. This is the work of conscious embodiment, finding a way to accept and include every aspect of ourselves and the totality of life as they really are.

A Reference Point and a Technique

In order to take the path of balance, I have found it helps to have reference points, both a kinesthetic one, which relates to sensations in our bodies, and a conceptual one, which relates to what we want to develop in ourselves. Together, they provide coordinates along which our minds and hearts can move and a way to embody the sensations that surge through our being. They create a context for the self that is both solid and flexible, allowing for dynamic change without getting lost.

These reference points help us stabilize when the truth of our dark side or our light side becomes unbearable. By this I mean that as we start to grow, we soon discover that either we cannot stand the fear, aggression, shame, or other destructive emotions that surface, or we cannot stand the softness, love, connectedness, or intimacy that comes with our truth. To actualize conscious embodiment, we need to be able to tolerate our aloneness and our belonging. When it becomes too difficult, we can apply a technique that allows us to rest and stabilize. I call this technique "basic practice," which focuses our attention on our breath, field, and the sensation of gravity. Next, we choose a quality associated with our vision of what we want to embody. The quality is given a name, a word like "openness," "compassion," "acceptance," or "courage." Our quality represents a forward movement of our spirit, and by moving toward something, we embrace life.

Into the Present

By cultivating our concentration for staying with our sensations, we develop a kind of strength which enables us to stay in the present. As we begin to feel these sensations, there is a tendency to move into the past or future when any physical or emotional pressure arises. It takes time, perseverance, and courage to keep returning to the present, to the feeling of life in the moment, being just here, just now, with this breath and this sense of gravity.

When we begin to be able to settle into the present, we can experience what is often called "the Mystery"—life unfolding in its infinite flux. If we are in the future or the past, we miss the present, the subtleties, the nuances, and the shifts of intensity. Our systems can no longer respond accurately because they are either stuck in a loop from the past or busy obsessing with the energy of some projected future. Even if our memories of the past or our ideas of the future are correct, the present is still missed.

Training ourselves to feel the present is like an acquired taste. Our first experiences of the present may not be so palatable. But as we keep tasting the present, over time we begin to like all aspects, including the simplicity, the bitterness, and the richness. Who knows, maybe the present will become our favorite flavor. Perhaps we can penetrate through our cultural biases of approval and control and begin to be, allowing our lives to unfold. Rather than creating the self-fulfilling prophecies of "I knew it would turn out like that," we could experience amazement, happiness, sadness, fear, delight, or any of the other feelings of our humanness. Instead of saying to ourselves, "If only so and so would do this and that, I would be okay," we can be responsible for ourselves in the present.

Learning to come to the present involves a sense of gathering ourselves together. We gather ourselves out of the the general fragmentation in which we live most of the time, where we try to cover both the past and the future simultaneously. This process can be strengthened by giving our attention different focal points. As we keep coming back to these focal points, our attention becomes more and more concentrated.

Coming into Sensation

Coming into the present is coming into sensation. To make the present compelling, we can focus on our breath in a particular way and follow it as it spirals through our body. We can explore our field by checking its front, back, left, right, above, and below. Sensing gravity first as pressure on our feet and buttocks, we can then move on to the weight of our internal organs, or head, or hands. Perhaps we can hear sound current, the sound that can be heard when things become very quiet. We do this as much as possible without watching or observing ourselves.

We want to be, to become the sensation. The only time we want to use the observer is to notice that we have shifted to the future or the past. Sometimes the sensation is that of stillness. When we become totally still, as when we are watching a movie or a play that is so riveting, there is no restlessness. Our total attention is focused on the moment. We are completely open to what will come; we are fascinated and full of curiosity.

This, to me, represents the female or *yin* side of being—the experience of not doing, of holding the space for the unfolding process. That quietness and receptivity allows something that represents the male or *yang* side of the experience to emerge. We have an insight or feel a strong sensation of energy moving through our bodies. We may go with it for a while and then we return to the space, the not doing. The more we practice, the more familiar not doing becomes, and it can become a place of refuge. We can take refuge from obsessive thoughts of future or past as we learn to rest in the quietness and become stable.

Knowing the River

Our life experiences can be very much like river rafting. There are times when we can let ourselves be carried by the river. We can take our paddles out of the water and relax and enjoy the scenery. Then there are times when we are running whitewater rapids and we need to paddle. We have to use every bit of ourselves to keep the boat on the proper line, otherwise we may be flipped in a hole or wrapped around a rock.

When we have explored our perceptions and inner life, we can anticipate certain reactions from ourselves. We may have to work to avoid calamities of our own doing. Metaphorically, this is like knowing the river—we know that a certain rapid has particular dangers so we paddle and work skillfully with them. Inevitably, there are times when we get dunked. We get out of the water, get back in the raft, and continue on our journey.

An eddy is a change in the river current, usually along the bank, where the water moves backward or in reverse to the flow of the river, creating a spiral in the water. Eddies, like all phenomena, can either be useful or become traps. We can use eddies as places to hang out in and wait. Sometimes, kayackers use them to go back upriver to ride the rapid again. When we get stuck in an eddy it can be very frustrating. Everyone else is floating by and we are going around and around and not making any progress along the river. Every time we try to row out we get sucked back in. Sound familiar? The skill in getting out of an eddy is knowing how to read the water, being able to see the precise place in the rippling current where, with some effort, we can get ourselves back into the mainstream.

Knowing when and how to get ourselves back into the mainstream comes from experience: knowing ourselves and knowing the river. Some of the knowing comes from our capacity for perception, the ability to see, feel, or hear the right time, the exact place. This perception comes from the practices I described earlier and will present in more detail later in the book. Conscious embodiment is the manifestation of our capacity to stay in the present, to hold the space of the moment, and to be with our body sensations, which enhances our ability to see and navigate skillfully.

> "So-This-is-a-River!"
> "The River," corrected the Rat.
> "And you really live by the River? What a jolly life."
> "By it and with it and on it and in it," said the Rat. "It's brother and sister to me, and aunts, and company, and food and drink and (naturally) washing. It's my world and I don't want any other. What it hasn't got isn't worth having, and what it doesn't know isn't worth knowing."
> —Kenneth Grahame, *The Wind in the Willows*

Chapter Two

The Elements of Basic Practice

It has been said that if you don't have discipline, it is like try-
ing to walk without legs. You cannot obtain liberation without
discipline.

Chögyam Trungpa

In order to get our bearings and begin to move in a more directed
fashion, we need a reference point. Since embodied action is one
of our goals, I use a reference point based on body sensations. We
can develop this reference point with what I call basic practice. The
techniques of basic practice help us focus our attention on body sensations. By using our sensations as a reference point, we are able to
cultivate our bodily intuition or clairsentience. Over time, with continuous practice, we strengthen our capacity to accept or tolerate
these sensations. Instead of evaluating situations in terms of being
bad or good, we experience quantities of energy. We can measure
the situation in terms of pressure, textures, and pulsations. As our
capacity grows through practice, we can receive more and more
information while staying centered enough to use the information
constructively.

The fact that we need to develop strength to tolerate being awake
and present may be a little surprising to some. But, in my years of
teaching, I have discovered that we have to strengthen our attention,
our breath, and our sense of balance in order to interact skillfully
with each situation as it arises. Skillfully interacting with the situa-

tion means that we can be open to and interested in what is occurring in any moment of our lives.

Basic practice draws us into the present and gives us a way to develop a relationship with ourselves based on being awake from moment to moment. Our tendency is to attempt to anticipate what might occur so that we will have no surprises; we feel in control because we think we know what will happen in advance. Paradoxically, what we need to do is not know in advance. We want to be able to be in the organic unfolding process. This practice gives us a way to gather and collect our attention over and over again until the act becomes easy and familiar. We want our ability to focus our attention to be strong and toned like a well-developed muscle so that we can easily and willingly return to the present and hold the sensations of our breath, gravity, and our energetic field.

Confidence comes from doing something over and over to the point where we feel we can do it naturally. As we develop our ability to return to ourselves, our confidence begins to develop and this way of being becomes very "do-able." As we persist in our practice, returning to ourselves becomes familiar, and we begin to think, "This is the way I am." If we lose ourselves for a moment, we feel confident that our training will allow us to shift back to the reference point. This can be described as spiritual confidence, the capacity to do what is one step beyond our capacity to know.

The spontaneous unfolding of situations is more interesting, satisfying, and empowering if we are energetically present in them. With basic practice, we are particularly interested in focusing ourselves in terms of sensation, because sensation intrinsically connects us to the present. By using sensation as a reference point we can perceive situations in terms of the amount, or intensity, of their energy versus our judging them as being good or bad. The key to this work is building an ability to perceive, tolerate, or accept energy in our systems. The more we stabilize ourselves and allow sensations to occur, the more we can interact directly and intuitively without reflexively trying to control the situation through our intellect.

A Centering Triad: Three Parts of Attentional Concentration

When we realize that we are in a reactive state, we can use basic practice to give ourselves a stable self to return to. Most people readily identify with the aspect of themselves that is in desire or anxiety in relationship to either the past or the future. In order to take hold of our lives, we have to experience the difference between living in a reactive, unbalanced state and being present in a centered self. When we are angry, afraid, critical, or in fantasy states, we are in reaction. Our reactive self is very articulate and compelling, with clear pictures, dialogues, and sensations.

How can we develop a self to come back to that is as magnetic as the reactive self? By using the same techniques as our neuroses, those of dialogue, sensations, and pictures. We use these techniques to develop a defined positive self to come home to so we can stabilize and open ourselves to the potential of the present moment. There are three parts to the technique of basic practice: breath, balance, and gravity.

Utilizing Our Breath

Many meditation practices and relaxation techniques utilize the breath as a way to focus attention. The part of the breath that we focus on in basic practice is the exhale. We use the exhale to direct our attention down toward either the *hara,* a point in the center of the belly two or three inches below the navel, or toward the center of the earth. Making an audible exhale and sustaining it for as long as possible makes this experience interesting enough to hold our attention. With our imagination we can enhance our interest in the experience. For example, using visualization, we could imagine a sun in our belly, and when we breathe into our belly the sun begins to glow brighter.

What we experience, when our breath leads us to a state that feels more embodied, can take many forms. The following experiences of three students illustrate the diversity of what we can experience.

My experience is an auditory one. I hear the breath and then I become it. I become the bumpiness of it. I'm able to smooth out the bumps through the hearing of it. From the sound of my breath, I'm able to adjust the kinesthetic experience of it. When I hear my breath go *"ahh-uhhh ahh u-hhh,"* I then can adjust it and make it go *"ahhhhhhhhh."*

—Alicia

When I focus on my breath I get serious. It is as if focusing on my breath is really important and my thoughts stop racing and wandering. What follows is a kinesthetic experience that started as a mental focusing with the message to really pay attention. The message comes from my morality, an intuitive prioritizing of sorts, which takes me to the kinesthetic experience, and then I am in it.

—Edward

When I exhale my attention first shifts to my throat. I experience great pressure in my throat from a semi-tightened glottis. When I feel this tightness, it is my signal use the sound the *"ahhhhhhhhh."* Using this breath creates an auditory awareness that drops my attention into my belly.

—Barbara

Balancing Our Energy Field

Each of our bodies is surrounded by an energy field. Scientifically it can be measured as an amount of heat emanating from the body, and it represents our energetic relationship to our surrounding environment. To experience our field, we begin by bringing our attention to our body. In the field itself there are a variety of personal experiences; moreover, the field size can vary dramatically. In this culture we are generally more frontal in our energy field, as vision is our dominant mode of perception. This frontal approach is apparent when we see people lean forward when talking, walking, or sitting.

The way we most frequently see ourselves is by looking into a bathroom mirror. This limited perspective can also become our energetic view of ourselves: we only experience the flat, topmost, and frontal part of our field while we ignore our back and lower body. To regain a more unified experience of ourselves, the second aspect of basic practice is a question: "Is the front of my field even to the back?"

In asking this question, our attention is drawn to our back, and for a moment more energy is brought to it. The mind is asking the body a question. The answer will usually be "no," but that is not the point of the question: we are asking for a sensate response. In asking the question, our attention and energy have made a shift, and in the process more balance occurs. When the shift occurs in our body, it can emanate into our field. This practice is different from telling ourselves to straighten up. We are trying to arouse our interest in sensation rather than ordering ourselves into a particular state.

Rather than giving a direction, we are open to what may occur. We let go of any preconceived ideas left over from yesterday or a minute ago. We ask the question, "Is the front of my field equal to the back?" and the implication is, "What would that be like?" After we have asked the question, we pause to feel the response in sensation.

Feeling Gravity

The third part of the centering triad is gravity. We can shift our attention to the sensation of gravity at any time. Once again we approach this element with a question: "Can I feel the sensation of gravity in my body?" We all weigh a certain amount. When we try to lift our own weight, we know it is substantial. It is a grounding experience to take a moment and sense our actual weight. In this exercise we can explore the variety of experiences of gravity in relationship to our bodies. We can inquire about the weight of our arms, our internal organs, and our head. Using my imagination helps me to explore the sense of weight in my body. For example, sometimes I imagine the molecules in my body. When I have a clear feeling of them, I imagine the particles in them suddenly falling to the bottom of the molecules. This intensifies my experience of grounding.

Practicing the Technique

In using the technique of basic practice, we collect and focus ourselves around basic body-oriented reference points: breath, balance of field, and sensation of gravity. The breath is a long exhale focused downward toward our *hara* or the center of the earth. We explore the balance of our field by asking a question, "Is the front of my field equal with the back?" And, we explore the sensation of gravity with the question, "Can I feel the weight of my body?"

Where and when do I do basic practice? I do it standing in line. I do it when I'm walking. I do it when I'm waiting for the light to change. In other words, I integrate it into the many gaps that occur in my life. Basic practice can be part of a personal practice. This practice can also be a centering resource in times of personal stress.

Our attention is often like a puppy, running around chewing on everything in sight. By lovingly calling it back to our side again, the puppy learns to come and sit quietly by our side. By shifting our attention to the elements of basic practice, we train ourselves to experience unification and presence.

Personalizing Basic Practice

One of the elements that makes basic practice so powerful is that it can be personalized. We have not borrowed it from anyone so it cannot be taken back or away. As we develop this practice, by changing it here and there, or concentrating on one aspect more than another for awhile, we begin to make it a personal practice. To be compelling enough to hold our attention, our practice must touch our hearts; we really have to feel it. It must interest our mind, and our mind needs to be willing to move from one aspect to another. We need to sense that it is a real experience. That is, we can get up, move around, and do a task while in this state. It is important that our practice does not become mechanical.

The living quality of basic practice can be detected through sensation—we can feel our presence: the weight or lightness of our body, the texture and size of our field, the length and depth of our breath. We become tuned into ourselves and can detect the subtle shifts in texture and intensity as we move from a thought to a sensation, from talking internally to listening internally, from sending a sensation to receiving a sensation.

Basic practice develops our ability to coach ourselves. We can develop a language to communicate with ourselves. We learn when to support and when to push. This is the spiritual side of our internal dialogue, as opposed to the neurotic side, which berates, criticizes, or whines. We want to develop and strengthen the voice of our spiritual coach. We can become interested in finding new and interesting ways to encourage and inspire ourselves. This is why we have teachers. We can pick up ideas from them, try them on, and adjust them to ourselves. What works for one person does not necessarily work for another, but sometimes it may be just the thing.

When I trained horses, I would try to get the horse to move in a precise way at an exact speed and respond to very subtle movements of my hands, legs, and posture. Evenness was very important. As the horse would trot and canter in circles and figure eights around the ring, I would chant, "Easy—eeea-sy" under my breath to the horse. In retrospect, I think it was to myself as well.

Years later, when I began aikido, my teacher, Robert Nadeau, used to demonstrate his own process of preparing for a throw. He would say "eeea-sy, eeea-sy," drawing the sound of the "eee" out as if to slow himself down so he would not rush the timing. The memory and synchronicity of these two events reassured my senses that I had come home, back again, to the training ground. Only this time, it was more obvious that I was really training myself toward the same evenness I had always sought in my horses. For someone else, even me at another time, eea-sy might be a way of not putting my whole self into it. It might be a cop-out. We have to explore the technique for ourselves and find out what is needed at a particular time.

Since we have so many wonderful teachers available to us through books, classes, and seminars, we have plenty of ideas to choose from. The important thing is to stay current and in touch with our internal coach. We must ask, "Is my self-coaching really supportive? Am

I with myself at this time?" Our interest is the key. As long as we are interested, the information will be forthcoming. However, we have to be willing to explore and try on different approaches, so that we can find something that inspires us where we are now.

Practicing and Accepting the Mystery

The living quality of basic practice must be nurtured and fed with interest and curiosity. Miyamoto Musashi, Japan's most famous sixteenth-century swordsman, once said, "The purpose of today's training is to defeat yesterday's understanding." Instead of clinging to some idea or insight with a rigid death grip, we can have the courage to release what we previously knew and either learn it again as a fresh insight, or perhaps allow a completely different insight to rise in its place. The impoverished attitude of rigidly holding on to an insight or idea leads to a righteous and stiff style of behavior.

The willingness to wonder, to "not know," in the sense of being *willing to know* or *about to know*, opens the gate for natural, organic insights to arise. Sometime ago, when I was in Santa Fe, New Mexico, I did an inner process known as a Shaman Journey. Through guided imagery, dialogue, and listening to a drumming tape, I went on a deep internal journey.

During this journey, I met and interacted with different parts of myself and had a visualization of a Zen *roshi*, or teacher. He said, "I will show you how to hold the truth," and handed me a cup of tea in an even and very precise manner. After he held his cup for a moment, he added, "and then you have to . . . ," as he threw his cup up in the air where it disappeared, "throw it away!" and he laughed a big belly laugh. Hold the truth carefully and then throw it away.

We greatly challenge our Western habit of getting, holding, keeping, and answering when instead, we release to curiosity, opening, and asking. Yet it is entirely possible to do this with the willingness to bring ourselves back to the questions and elements of basic practice again and again. When we can return to our practice, that is great, because our training and capacity for discipline have helped us. When we cannot return to our practice, that is also great, because we know we need more training and practice in order to return to our reference point. Conscious embodiment is not a credential to grasp after, but rather an ongoing process, a whole-life process, a way of being present and interested in life's nuances.

Training ourselves to feel the nuances in the stillness of life is part of the maturing process. Our minds can be like a puppy sniffing and biting on every little fear or desire, easily seduced and distracted, wandering from one thought to another. What a nice experience it is when we can ask our puppy-mind to heel, to come back and sit quietly by our side. Usually we are out sniffing around, chewing, and biting. Through basic practice, we can begin to bring ourselves back, we can heel, so to speak, for a moment by sitting quietly with ourselves, reconnecting with our breath, feeling the weight and the size of our presence, and being available to perceive subtle changes as they occur.

With basic practice we begin a maturing process, which is really coming around full circle. When we were children, we were open and interested in exploring life. Life was a great mystery. Now as we settle back into ourselves, life can once again become a great mystery. We can abandon our attempts to conquer or control life and instead become part of the adventure while we are touched by and fascinated with being present in the moment as it is.

Chapter Three

Adding a Quality

*Little by little, we change the world we live in. Even the grand,
earth-shaking events of history have their origins in individual thought.*

Eknath Easwaran

When I first began meditating, sitting still and watching my
breath rise and fall, I was dismayed by the amount of negativity I experienced when I lost my concentration on my breath. As
soon as my attention wandered, which was often, I was confronted
by anger, guilt, and sadness. The idea of going into myself to become
centered was ridiculous. How could I become centered if every time
I focused my attention inward I hated myself? I felt stymied. Visualization helped at times, but it could not begin to balance the intensity of my negative identification with life. I needed to find some
way to connect with myself in a positive way.

I began using a Buddhist meditation called *metta,* which means
"loving-kindness." It is a powerful practice in which the practitioner
makes a request in the form of, "May I be _____." Tradition-
ally, the meditator requests, "May I be happy. May I be peaceful.
May I be liberated." The concept of liberation seemed too big for
me so I substituted, "May I be filled with love." *Metta* is a three-lay-
ered practice. After beginning with oneself, the same requests are
asked for loved ones, then awareness is expanded to make the request

for all sentient beings, and ends with a return to oneself, asking, "May I be happy. May I be peaceful. May I be filled with love."

During a particularly difficult period, I used the *metta* practice countless times every day to counter the rage and hatred I was feeling. Slowly my inner life began to quiet down as the *metta* steadied me. I realized that I really wanted to be helpful to people, and that in order to be more helpful, I wanted to cultivate more softness in my being. At some point, it occurred to me that if I substituted my own words in the *metta* practice, it would become more my own. I began to say, "I wish to have more softness, give more love, and be of greater service." At times even this request seemed too demanding, so I modified the practice even more, asking, "If there were more softness in my being, what would that feel like?" Framing my request as a question captured my interest, instead of triggering my resistance. Asking a question allowed me to explore the experience of having a positive quality in my being.

Why a Quality?

Most of us have not yet arrived at the place where we can maintain our balance throughout all life situations. Our reactive self usually has a strong identity, and like well-developed muscles in a dominant arm, tends to intensify some situations. Just as we need to strengthen the nondominant arm for physical balance, we need to strengthen our centered selves for energetic balance. Using basic practice strengthens our centering abilities. We also need to develop a positive experience of ourselves for psychic and emotional balance. And, we can nurture a positive experience with ourselves by adding a quality to our basic practice. Our quality provides a focus and helps us stabilize our emotional center.

We invoke our quality by asking the question, "What would it be like if I had more _____?" We fill in the blank with the quality we want to embody. The question could also be phrased, "If I could have more _____ in my life, what would that feel like?" As the wording of this question implies, the quality is something we want to have more of in our being. So, it is important that the quality we choose is something we already possess yet want to develop further.

Identifying a Quality

Our neuroses are very articulate about the experiences we might desire. We can have elaborate internal dialogues about the negative attributes we want to relinquish. But when we focus our attention on what we want to enrich in ourselves, our internal voice is often at a loss for words. By choosing a quality that we have felt before and want to feel more of, we strengthen and cultivate a positive aspect of ourselves that already exists.

Openness, clarity, acceptance, appreciation, gentleness, tenderness, and affection are some of the qualities that I have chosen over the years to cultivate in myself. Aliveness, groundedness, depth, love, compassion, trust, and intimacy are but a few examples of qualities that conscious embodiment students have chosen over the years. The quality we choose needs to be something that creates a strong response in our emotional center. Our quality can be difficult to feel if it is too abstract. Alternatively, our quality can be overpowering if it is so charged that we start crying as soon as we evoke it. An effective quality is one that, in any moment, is absolutely appropriate to possess.

It is important to avoid choosing a quality based on a "should," such as "I should be softer" or "I should be more dynamic." The word "should" indicates an internal demand that usually comes from a concept or an idea of what we think we ought to be. Going into "should" territory usually puts our system into resistance. As a consequence, we may not feel anything when we evoke our quality or we might find that we just do not want to be bothered with it.

We may be able to instantly identify a quality we want to nourish or we may need to search for the most appropriate one for our circumstances. In both situations, it is helpful to "try on" the quality before we commit to working with it over time. After we evoke

a quality by asking the question," What would it be like if I had more
_____?", we wait for a sensation to arise in response. If no sensation surfaces, we can try another quality or word.

Some qualities are so advanced or expansive that we can sabotage ourselves if we attempt them prematurely. Be careful of qualities such as "peace" or "joy." It is likely that we could find ourselves in situations where it would be very difficult to access the feeling of peace or joy.

Using the Body as the Teacher

In addition to cultivating a positive identity, evoking a quality brings an additional benefit: the mind becomes the student while the body is the teacher. For instance, if our quality is "tenderness," the mind would ask the body: "If there were more tenderness in my being, what would that feel like?" We are particularly interested in sensations, but we will accept information of any kind—inner voices, and pictures as well. The mind is receptive, the student, and the body is positive, the teacher. This is an important shift in our baseline perception.

In the time between our asking the question and receiving information, we are in a state of openness and "not-knowing." This "not-knowing" is the state from which creativity and intuition arise. If we already have a mental idea of what the answer will be to the question we are asking, then there is no space for an intuitive impression to arise. When we evoke our quality, we want to take the attitude that we have no idea what the response will be. And, besides, there is no absolutely correct answer for us ultimately to uncover. To open the space for creativity and intuition to arise, we want to approach each instance with interest and fascination and not assume that we know what our inner response will be.

A Centerpiece for Practice

Our quality can become the centerpiece to our basic practice because it has the capacity to create intense physical and emotional moments of personal intimacy. Our quality can hook our attention to ourselves in the present moment. We can begin to use our quality as a reference point and as a means to stabilize our relationship with ourselves.

For many years now, I have chosen a different quality, one word, every Fall. I work with each quality for one year. Identifying a different quality is the beginning of a new journey with myself. I usually have a set of ideas about what the quality will bring, but as the weeks and months pass, having asked and evoked the quality many times, unexpected responses begin to occur. Inevitably, I discover previously hidden dimensions of myself. Not only do I learn to deepen my capacity for the quality I have chosen, but more importantly I stimulate my curiosity and enter the mystery again and again.

Chapter Four

Energy and Stability

I have not a shadow of a doubt that any man or woman can achieve what I have, if he or she would make the same effort and cultivate the same hope and faith.

Gandhi

What are the components that create or enhance stability in something? What makes a tree, a house, a tent, or a car stable? What do we do to keep something from falling over or collapsing? There are, of course, many possibilities, but one key principle is to strengthen the base—the foundation or root system. Sometimes it is a matter of widening the base, sometimes we deepen the base, and sometimes reinforcing the base is helpful.

Human beings are much more dynamic than houses or cars. Like a plant, whose root system must be nourished to insure the growth and productivity of its limbs, we must engage in constant and subtle maintenance to keep our centering or energetic base strong, well-toned, and vibrant. We can use our attention to achieve more stability and enhance our sense of contact with our base.

Learning to direct our attention empowers us. When our attention is focused and unified, our capacity to function becomes heightened. In fact, phenomenal events can occur. We have all heard the stories of grandmothers who pick up cars to rescue babies or of young boys who lift tractors off their trapped fathers. Energy is like light. When it is diffused it has a pleasant feeling. When energy is focused, it is like a laser, the strongest tool known to us. We have the capacity both to diffuse and to concentrate our energy.

Energy Follows Attention

Energy tends to go where there is the most excitement, most clarity, most intensity. Energy follows attention. Wherever we focus our attention, our energy follows. By focusing our attention, we can stabilize ourselves. There are times in our lives when we feel inspired and know what we want. At other times, we are confused and scattered. During those insecure times, we can arbitrarily choose some quality to steady ourselves and shift our attention.

In addition to establishing a basic neutral stability, one of the first steps on a path is being able to say what we want and what we are moving toward. For most people, those who are not on a path and those who have not positively trained themselves, the focus of attention and energy is drawn to their negative aspects. In using basic practice and adding a quality, we are shifting our attention toward being centered and having stability.

An experience of a beginning student illustrates how energy follows attention:

> When I first started taking Wendy's class, I was training for a rowing competition. I am a power versus endurance athlete, and I was very focused on my lack of stamina. While rowing, I often heard an inner voice hysterically chanting, "I don't have any stamina." I would offer this negative mantra as a self-appraisal when discussing my rowing with others.
>
> Walking home from work one day, I was thinking about my lack of stamina and it hit me: "Energy follows attention!" Then I asked, "What am I doing to myself?" As of that day, I began to ask, "What would it be like if I had more endurance?" Because I was so physically engaged while rowing, I would register a sensation in my body in response to the question.
>
> As my training progressed, I evoked additional qualities while rowing. Asking "What would it be like if I had more power?" liberated untapped reserves. The most important

gain, however, was knowing that I could break free from the panic that could suddenly consume me on the water.

—Kevin

Embellishing Our Centering Practice

Energy follows attention: whatever we put our attention on develops and grows. Our neuroses can be quite versatile and distract us in many ways. They can be in vivid technicolor images, or they can be associated with and evoked by certain sounds and smells. Our neuroses tell stories about us being the best or the worst. They can tell us we are right and the other person is wrong or the reverse, that someone is right and we are wrong. The "if only" style of neurosis tells stories about what we might have done. Our neuroses often have an obsessive quality, like a needle stuck in a groove of a record, repeating the same line over and over again.

Focusing our attention and staying with our centering practice is difficult when we have all those wild scenarios going on internally. This difficulty is just the reality of our practice. It is as if we are in a room with a gigantic, technicolor movie screen controlled by our neuroses and below the screen is a tiny black-and-white television showing our centering practice. Both are competing for our attention. It is hard to watch that little television when the large, bright screen can so easily distract us. Part of the challenge, then, is to embellish our centering practice in any way that makes it interesting enough to hold our attention.

We need to be creative in coming back to ourselves. The more energy we can add to our practices, the more we can get involved in the richness of being back in ourselves. We can ask about our breath, our field, and the sensation of gravity. The goal is to keep our attention at home. Basic practice, for example, can be practiced as a quick and simple technique to collect and stabilize ourselves, and it can be also be elongated and developed into a meditation practice to engage our attention for longer periods of time. I have developed a personalized meditation from basic practice which uses a spiral breath to cleanse and strengthen my energy.

A Spiral-Breath Meditation

I begin by imagining that the bottoms of my feet are open, and that energy from the earth can be received through them. As I inhale, I imagine that I am drawing energy from mother earth. The in-breath moves in a counterclockwise direction. When I exhale, the breath is clockwise, moving back into the earth. The inhale is associated with cleansing or purifying. The exhale is associated with strengthening or empowering.

I use nine areas in my body to focus my breath. At each area, I take between one and five complete breaths to cleanse and strengthen that particular area. The number of breaths depends upon my sense of the strength or health of the particular area as well as my ability to focus. If I am feeling scattered, I use three to five breaths to help gather my attention in a particular area. When I lose my concentration in any area, I start that area again or do extra breaths to bring my awareness back into focus.

I begin the spiral-breath meditation with an inhale, drawing the breath through the bottoms of my feet and taking a counterclockwise turn at the ankles. I think of this part of the breath as cleansing the ankle joints. When I exhale, I focus my breath turning back through the ankles again, this time in a clockwise direction. I move to the knee joints, and imagine my breath spiraling there. With each in-breath, I imagine that it is cleansing and purifying my knees. With each out-breath, I imagine it strengthening and empowering my knees. My attention moves to the floor of my pelvis and genital area as I repeat the same process: the inhale cleanses, the exhale strengthens. The next point is the *hara* or abdomen, where I repeat the process drawing the breath from the earth and spiraling it around my belly. After that I move to the solar plexus and continue the breathing pattern. From the solar plexus, I move up to the heart, then to the neck, then to the center of my head, behind my eyes. Finally, I draw the breath to the very top of my head and it spirals towards heaven. The exhale comes down from above, spiraling through my body and strengthening my whole being.

Having completed this part, I relax and allow my breath to flow naturally. Even though I am relaxed, I still retain an awareness of the purifying inhale moving counterclockwise and the strengthening exhale moving clockwise.

After being with my breath in this relaxed way for awhile, I sit as if I am about to hear or feel or see something: the "not-knowing" state. If I see, hear, or feel something, I note it and return to the state of openness. I find this state helpful for suspending any agenda I might have in regards to the next moment.

When I feel it is the time for ending the meditation, I reorient to my breath. I inhale spiraling up, cleansing, and exhale spiraling down, strengthening. I check the perimeter of my field in all directions: in front, behind, to the left and right, above and below. Then I shift my attention to the sensations of heaviness or lightness. I spend a moment evoking my quality. At this point, I open my eyes and I get up and move around. Sometimes the feeling or experience of the meditation will stay with me, other times it falls away.

With regular practice, our centered experiences will increase and become a vital functioning part of ourselves. These experiences can balance us while helping us to tolerate and accept the aspects of ourselves that make us uncomfortable. Meditation practice gives us ground from which we can openly face and work with ourselves. It is ritual in the sense that we bring ourselves to it with intention. We repeat the practice in order to gather and strengthen the energy pattern. It is both sacred and ordinary—we practice in an ordinary manner the sacred concentration of being in the moment.

Take Your Time

The universe is dynamic; its energy is always pushing on us. As soon as we are able to manage one aspect of our lives, another challenge is offered as an opportunity to grow. Rather than hoping to remain stable once and for all, our goal is to stabilize momentarily. To clarify this, O Sensei said, "It is not that I don't get off center. I correct so fast that no one can see me." The idea is to become skilled at coming back, not holding on. The benefit comes from developing our ability to return. The more we practice returning to center, the more we can center in everyday situations.

When we are unified and able to experience ourselves as powerful, it is sometimes frightening. Feeling powerful may become an identity crisis. There is a tendency to sabotage ourselves and move back to our old pattern because it is familiar. As appealing as the idea of unification seems, being able to tolerate and embody the actual experience is a long-term, whole-life practice.

I encourage the acceptance of longevity with this kind of practice and training. There is nothing instantaneous about it. The insights might be instant, but there is a difference between having an insight and living an insight. If insight were enough, then all the people who take hallucinogenic drugs or write books on personal development would be happy, together, and enlightened. They are not. Having insight does not lead to an embodied experience. In fact, it can be incredibly painful to gain an insight and then have our body react in a different way. We need to recognize that conscious embodiment is a long-term process that is integrated into our daily lives.

Establishing a formal practice has been very helpful to me. It is formal in the sense that I practice every day, at predetermined times. I stop and bring my attention to my breath; sense my field in the front, back, left, right, above, and below; pay attention to the sensations of gravity; and then I evoke my quality.

For anyone interested in developing conscious embodiment, I recommend establishing a routine basic practice, three times a day at fixed times. For example, upon arising, going to bed, and some other time during the day. If meal times are regular, before or after meals are viable options. For me, the morning is the best time to sit down and practice the spiral-breath meditation. It sets the tone for the day and it can be worked into my schedule by getting up earlier.

A ritual meditation practice is essential to conscious embodiment. We agree to meditate for a specific amount of time: three, five, ten minutes or more. It is crucial to pick an amount of time that is feasible. Our practice has to be manageable, something we can do. It takes time to build and train a meditation practice.

Practice is the essential part of our spiritual growth. In order to earn a high-school diploma, a certain amount of time has to be invested. In order to reap the benefits of quieting our minds through meditation, we must devote a certain amount of time and effort each day to the practice. Worthwhile things take time. It takes time to strengthen our muscles, build a house, or get a Ph.D. Yes, it does take time, but if we do the work, we will see the benefits: a strong capable body, a house to live in, and a doctoral degree. We must begin sometime. *Today is the perfect day.*

Chapter Five

Learning

It has been said, quite accurately, that a psychotic person is drowning in the very same things that a mystic swims in.

Pema Chödrön

Recently someone asked me, "Why do we learn?" It was such a good question that I stopped to consider it for quite awhile. I invite you to stop reading for a moment and consider the questions:

Why do we learn?

What is learning based on—survival? control? inspiration? curiosity?

What is it in our humanness that seeks to surpass itself?

There seems to be a very deep and primitive drive connected with the act of learning. More than any other creature, a human will work endlessly to increase physical ability or capacity for life. Some of us will train tirelessly in order to be able to run faster, leap higher, throw farther, and stretch beyond our limits.

What is it that our spirit hungers for? Where are we trying to go? Or perhaps the question might be: What are we trying to get away from? It is always challenging for me to ponder these questions. Often I receive some answers, but ultimately these are only bits and pieces. The important element in learning is in asking the questions. After asking the question, we wait and listen and then we can get answers. The process is ongoing: we wait a while and receive more answers then we ask again, wait, and listen.

The magnetic pull that draws our spirit toward increasing our capacity for life creates the process of learning. *Webster's Dictionary* says that to learn is "to gain knowledge, comprehension, or mastery through experience or study." So, how do we get the experience? How do we study?

Approaches to Learning

The martial arts are among many disciplines with diverse theories on the stages of learning and how to develop a skill. A teacher of *iaido,* the art of Japanese sword drawing and cutting, tells his students, "first you have to be able to make the movement big, then strong, then quick, then light."

Another teacher of sword and aikido draws a metaphor in the body. "The first level is like bone, hard and solid. The second level is like flesh, still solid but more moveable. The next level is like blood, fluid and liquid. The next level is like nerves, tiny electrical impulses that fire the message. Finally there is breath; you can't see it but you can feel it and the effects of it."

Both of these teachers emphasize starting with a definite and solid kind of practice and then moving to a more refined subtle approach. I have also studied with teachers who advocate the opposite, starting soft and easy, and, over time, building up to strong and powerful. When I trained in Germany, some students were shocked that I grabbed them hard. To my surprise, they told me that no one ever grabbed hard until they reached brown belt, when they could begin to work with the stronger grips.

In my experience, the way we learn is a completely personal and individual experience. If we can become interested in the process and are willing to experiment with ourselves, our journey can be rich, exciting, and endless.

Interest versus Fear

In our culture and our educational system, learning is based on fear: the fear of failure. Failure is often associated with the fear that love and approval will be withdrawn. Even after our formal education is over, the fear habit is still in effect. We have developed a habit of associating learning with getting "F's"—the "inner F," when we fail ourselves, and the "outer F," when we are perceived as a failure by others. The self-hatred generated by the "inner F" is the basis for much of our unhappiness and aggression.

My estimate is that most people have been learning in an environment that is 70 to 90 percent fear and frustration with 10 to 30 percent interest. Our goal is to change the percentage so that interest and curiosity are more than 50 percent of our motivation.

The first step is to create and explore situations where we can study ourselves. If we slow down and really look, we can begin to notice what kinds of fear and aggression we have towards ourselves. We may see that we judge ourselves in comparison to others, and alternatively, that we judge ourselves according to some internal standards. Both result in our spending a lot of time spinning around in judgments. And instead of being interested and excited about learning, we get frustrated. We must study ourselves and our behavior to know how and when we go into our "fear of failure" routines.

The second step in reducing our fear percentage to less than 50 percent is to use techniques which appease our fears by acknowledging them. When we acknowledge our fears, we lessen our resistance to them because we are no longer trying to deny them. Our fears are not so easily engaged when there is nothing for them to push against like our resistance.

The third step is to stimulate our interest by asking what it would be like if we responded differently. When we pause to ask the question, we allow space for our curiosity to bloom. Our questions can awaken and cultivate our interest in the many options available to us.

Self-judgments will always arise, but we do not have to stay with them. During the time we are learning anything, there will be good moments, poor moments, pleasurable moments, and painful moments. Energy follows attention: the more attention we give to the poor and painful moments, the more frustrated we become. The more frustrated we become, the more we struggle and criticize ourselves, and train failure into our system. We do better when we can acknowledge all aspects, both "good" and "bad," and focus most of our attention on our interest and curiosity.

The Grinch and the "Yes, ... And, ..." Technique

When we begin any task, the energy to do the task enters our system. For example, imagine we are going to learn to do a new dance step: we focus our attention in our bodies and feel a rush of energy before we even begin to move. In addition to our desire to do well, the task of learning is also accompanied by our fear of not doing well. Consequently, we tighten our muscles and hold our breath to avoid feeling the process as we move quickly toward the end result. When we are tense or go ahead of the movement, the step is awkward and rough and the energy flow is blocked and uneven. Our internal critic, what I call the grinch, responds immediately, adding more energy laden with a negative judgment or criticism. The grinch might say, "That was lousy," or "I knew I would mess up." It is as if a cartoon bubble filled with a negative one-liner pops up every time we do something imperfectly.

The technique I have developed to work directly with my inner grinch is first to acknowledge its reaction and then ask a question. For example, my grinch says, "That was lousy." I reply, "*Yes,* that's true, it was lousy. *And,* if there were more smoothness in my body, what would it feel like?" This is what I call the "*Yes, ... And,...*" technique. By acknowledging the negative voice, we blend with it. We soften the negative blow by going with it and not resisting. Then we shift our attention by using the conjunction "and." Using "and" affirms that we can simultaneously hold our vision of how we want to perform without excluding our negative assessment. Asking the question leads our attention toward exploring the sensation of what we want to develop instead of fighting against our grinch.

Whenever I am learning or developing something, I expect negative comments to arise and I am ready for them. With practice, I have come to smile and acknowledge the familiar inner grinch that seizes any opportunity to harp on my limitations and inabilities. After all these years, I know the grinch is still there. This acknowledgment keeps me from being frustrated with myself.

I see the grinch as a flashing yellow light giving me a message: "Pay attention, there is energy on the move in your system." When I get this message, I focus on my sensations. I do not delve into the content of what the grinch has to say, but instead I choose to put my attention on the rush of energy in my body. From using the basic practice techniques, we know something about working with energy. When we feel the rush of energy or notice that we are tensing or speeding up, we can stop, focus on our breath, balance our energy field, feel gravity, and evoke our quality. When we stabilize and soften in this way, the energy can begin to self-organize in a way that allows us to deal with the situation more skillfully.

Whenever the negative critical voice of the grinch arises, go with it for a moment, make the blend, and use the *"Yes, ... And,..."* technique.

> *Yes*, that is true. *And*, if there were more *(your quality)* in my being, what would that feel like?

> Pause and feel any sensations that arise. A new perspective on the situation may come with the sensations.

Practice and Training

Great athletes keep surpassing themselves and each other. Their quest to achieve the next level or possibility becomes a way of life. For many athletes, this strength of spirit is represented in their willingness to stay interested and in their ability to be open to many possibilities. This kind of spirit leads to a life where practice and training are a natural and integrated way of being.

To develop our ability to do something, we have to train, practice, and strengthen through repetition, concentration, and presence. Repetition and concentration establish form. When this occurs, we no longer have to think about how to place our body or how to form a response. A new dimension begins to open up. Because we no longer have to focus our attention on the outer form, we are free to concentrate on the more subtle nuances of inner feelings, capacity, and timing.

Training generates momentum. If we practice on a regular basis, the habit of practicing can carry us through some of the times when we are more resistant and less inspired. It is like getting up enough speed on a bicycle so that when we get to a hill, the momentum carries us part of the way up. With momentum, going up the hill does not take as much effort as it does when we have not built up much speed.

Inspiration, spirit, and discipline are important factors in developing the habit of practicing. The ability to remain open and interested during practice keeps us present and our creativity alive. Otherwise, practice can become stiff, rigid, and dogmatic, and the creative unfolding quality of learning is lost.

Mistakes

There is a Chinese maxim about a seeker who climbs a very high mountain to ask the hermit sage about the meaning of life.

> *What is the most important aspect of one's life?*
> Experience.
> *How do you get experience?*
> Good judgment.
> *How do you get good judgment?*
> Bad judgment.

When we are engaged in the learning process, it is inevitable that we will make some mistakes. If we are using a particular form as a container to develop our potential, we strive to execute the form in a particular way. Our inability to do so may seem like a mistake, but a mistake is not so much a reflection of our inability as it is a signpost or opportunity to adjust. Our tendency is to react to the signpost in a negative way. When we spin a negative inner dialogue, we take time and energy away from the task at hand while the voice that criticizes splits us from our embodied selves. Using the *"Yes, ...*

And, . . . " technique helps us to shift our attention back to our sensations or to our quality.

When we reach the point in our training where we have achieved a sense of fluidity and enjoyment, a mistake can take on an entirely different meaning. When we are confident in ourselves and our form and we happen to make a mistake, that is, we do something that we did not intend to do, the mistake may lead to a new variation. Making a mistake can become a creative act. Mistakes are often a way for creativity to come through. A mistake can be the window to a deeper perception or wisdom.

It is important to recognize the difference between the mistakes we make when we are still learning the form and the mistakes that occur after the form is mastered. When we are still learning, our mistakes clearly result from our inexperience and inability to execute the form. After we have mastered the form and stay open to our process, we can use our mistakes as entries to new and creative ways of being within the form.

Filling in a Hole

Learning can be more like an exploration of new territory than a heavy-handed accumulation of knowledge and its associated illusion of power. Sometimes learning is a means of filling in a hole. Suppose that we have done something for twenty years and are proficient, fluid, and strong. Then something occurs in our relationship or job, perhaps we suffer a physical injury or we lose someone we love and this event triggers the realization that something is missing. Sometimes it is immediately clear what we are missing, and sometimes we have to uncover what we lack.

In the process of contacting and cultivating this missing piece, our whole system starts to shift and reorganize. This is a difficult period because it seems like everything is beginning to fall apart: everything seems to get worse before it gets better. It takes courage to be able to keep going despite our feelings of inadequacy. We have begun filling in the hole when instances of confidence return, we feel inspiration in our actions, and we start to feel excitement as insights arise and we embody them.

Learning is endless. In my personal system of semantics, I draw a distinction between an "elder" and an "old person" that corresponds to the capacity for learning. Elders are still immersed in learning about themselves and the wonders of the world. I have the good fortune of having some friends in their eighties and nineties who I consider to be elders. Their mental vitality and emotional delight in the learning process are a source of inspiration for me. One friend in particular, a very accomplished artist, says, "I may not have the greatest answers, but I can still ask some very good questions." When we practice conscious embodiment, we encourage ourselves toward a fascination with what is possible.

Part II

The Mind— Shaping Our Concepts

Chapter Six

The Spirit of Inquiry

"What do you like to do best in the world, Pooh?"
"Well," said Pooh, "What I like best—" and then he had to
stop and think.
Because eating honey was a very good thing to do. There
was a moment just before you begin to eat it, which was bet-
ter than when you were, but he didn't know what it was called.

A. A. Milne

The Habit of Interest

As our body becomes more stable from basic practice, we increase our capacity to accept and inquire into sensations. Practice develops a base from which we can observe and interact more adeptly with our mental process and thought patterns. As we are more able to focus on the movement of the mind, we begin to notice that there is a space between thoughts. This place of spaciousness is the womb of our creativity. From this still, calm place comes our inherent wisdom: the knowledge of our intuition with an understanding of what is needed for clear and compassionate action. The discipline of conscious embodiment allows us to penetrate the movement of the mind beyond our fears and desires.

Curiosity and interest can be stimulated in many ways. There is a man from India whose father and grandfather were world-famous musicians and considered the best sitar players of their time. Naturally, the father wanted his son to continue in the family tradition, but he did not want to force it on him—he wanted his son to make his own choice. To build his young son's desire to play, music was constantly played in the family home, but all instruments were kept out of the boy's reach. The boy was not even allowed to touch them. This situation aroused such interest and fascination in the boy that he ultimately begged to have an instrument. At some point the boy was given an instrument. And today, like his father and grandfather before him, this man is one of the most accomplished musicians of his time.

How can we cultivate our sense of interest to the point that it becomes a habit to be interested? When we are genuinely interested, we are not crowded in by thoughts of "what if," "I hope that," and "if only." Instead we are poised, soft, and open to what will arise. We are simply interested in life.

To have a directed interest, we have to collect our awareness into a single focused point of fascination. For most of us this is a great challenge. Usually we need to be furious or terrified to unify ourselves instantaneously. Our patterns for mobilizing ourselves are often based on either approval or achievement. Since the facility to unconditionally unify ourselves is not easily ingrained in our system, we need to develop the ability to focus our interest. We can strengthen our ability to focus just as we would build a muscle: through repetitious practice. At first, there will be no visible outcome or achievement, and no one is going to applaud us for our effort as we progress. *It is crucial that we practice just for the sake of the practice.*

The technique of asking ourselves a question and waiting for a response is my approach to conscious embodiment. Asking questions shifts our attention to the state of wonder, the place where our creativity and intuition arise.

The Fine Art of Questioning

Asking questions is an essential part of basic practice, evoking a quality, and the "Yes, ... And,..." technique. Questioning directs us toward an awareness of our sensations and feelings in the present. We ask questions that evoke our interest in sensation and bring us into an embodied experience in the present moment. Rather than evaluating situations in terms of being bad or good, we instead experience quantities of energy. We can measure the situation in terms of pressure, textures, and pulsations.

Asking questions is a means to sidestep our resistance. Therefore, we need to avoid questions which lead us into reactive behaviors such as withdrawal or aggression. It is important to explore our own internal semantics. Certain words resonate more positively for some people. What happens in our body when we use a particular word, such as "harmony," "strength," "humor," or "gentleness"? We want to find words that generate a strong sensate response, particularly when we are choosing a quality. It is often helpful to look up a word in the dictionary to stimulate our interest in its meanings.

There are also times when we may want to get information about an external situation. Asking, "What's happening?" usually floods our system with more information than it can handle. It is more manageable to break our inquiry into smaller parts. I often use a triad of questions, a technique first introduced to me by Helen Palmer. They are: "Where is the power or strength in the situation?" "Where is the weakness or the least amount of energy?" And, "What is the next step or what is needed?"

After each question, I wait in a state of openness and usually some response arises. In each case, I am interested in just a little piece of information. I do not need to get the whole story, past, and future. I only need what is true now, in the very moment. These pieces provide enough information to act skillfully in the next moment.

For instance, if someone in my workplace is behaving in a way that seems aggressive and competitive, I might ask, "Where is the strength?" Let us say that the intuitive impression I receive is that this person has a very strong, well-developed will, and forges ahead, ignoring pain in order to get the job done. In one sense, this strength means the person is very dependable. After centering and clearing the slate, I would ask, "Where is the weakness?" Now, perhaps, the intuitive impression I receive is that this person's heart-center seems contracted and threatened, making it difficult for him or her to access feelings of self or to take the feelings of others into account. My final question is, "What is needed?" A possible perception could be that more ground or stability would be helpful. A person who feels more grounded and stable can afford to tolerate feelings of self and behave in a more compassionate and balanced manner.

With the information I have received from asking these three questions, my challenge would be to give this aggressive person more support rather than resistance. With more support, this person would feel more stable and could afford to relax a little. This is conflict resolution instead of conflict retribution.

The Buoyant State of Curiosity

When we are genuinely interested, there is an openness in our being which allows space for answers and information to come to us. The habit of interest or curiosity can be developed with the repetition of basic practice. At first, we find that our mind quickly grasps at a response. Alternatively, we may quickly complain to ourselves that we have not gotten a response. In both situations, we need to recognize that we have fallen back into an approval or achievement state, and shift our attention back to the state of curiosity. It is the discipline of returning to the state of curiosity again and again that develops the capacity to hold or sustain it. Our practice is a matter of developing the ability to tolerate and hold the state of curiosity without grasping for an insight or getting distracted by the past or the future. If our curiosity is genuine, there is an openness or naiveté that allows a fresh point of contact with ourselves.

Buoyancy is a metaphor easily associated with this process of creating spaciousness in our being. We want to remain afloat in a sea where difficulties might drag us down. If we are so heavily weighted with our desire for the situation to be better, we are closed to discovering the options and we sink below the surface. When we are curious, we are soft and open to what may arise. For instance, when we do go underwater, we can begin our recovery by recognizing that we are in fact underwater. Likewise, if we get dragged down by a judgment or criticism about how we got into the situation, we can use the *"Yes, ... And, ..."* technique to acknowledge its truth and switch our focus to what we do want. We do not need to panic. With acknowledgment, focus, and a little effort, we can bring ourselves to the surface and inhale a nice breath of fresh air. The effort we expend is in the asking of a question. We can relate to each instant with precision and presence through our spirit of inquiry. This spirit of inquiry creates a sense of buoyancy because we no longer have the past or future weighing us down.

The Don't-Know Mind

One way to encourage intuition is to enter what Korean Zen master Sueng Sahn calls the "Don't-Know Mind." The "Don't-Know Mind" has space for the intuition to arise. It is important to remember that in order to develop curiosity and fascination as a way of being in the world, we have to concentrate on the curiosity itself and not let ourselves get seduced into the habit of grasping for answers. It is easy to have the illusion that understanding something will make everything better. If this were true, then the smartest people would be the happiest. We can see from those we know that this is definitely not the case. Happiness involves many other factors besides knowledge. The desire to know is a strong and motivating factor in our intellectual learning. The spiritual approach is to be able to take a completely fresh view of each moment. Even when we have an answer, it is only right for its moment, because the next moment is completely new.

Chapter Seven

Not-Knowing

The movement of the Way is a return;
In Weakness lies its major usefulness
From What-is all the world of things was born
But What-is sprang in turn from What-is-not.

Lao Tzu, *Tao Te Ching* #40

For thousands of years people have sought to understand the purpose of life. Great sages such as Lao Tzu and Confucius, philosophers like Plato and Aristotle, and brilliant religious leaders like Buddha and Christ, have all tried to explain the meaning of life. Yet with all of this valuable information, we still ask, "Who am I? Why am I here?" Maybe the questioning is the most important aspect, not the answers we receive. Asking the question can stimulate our fascination, which internally organizes us into a unified state of being, one without inner conflict.

This coming together of our being is in preparation for something. The expectation that something will occur puts our system in a state of readiness. Too often, in daily life, we miss this exquisite moment with its powerful spiritual quality. Instead, we fixate on the answer, the future, and our desire to control the outcome of the event. For me, the spiritual worth lies not in the answer but in the fantastic sense of readiness, the intense here and now of expectancy, the instant before we know, when we are still in a state of openness.

A Journey into Emptiness

The Buddhists have a term for what they consider to be the essence or central point of Buddhism: *shunyata,* usually translated as "emptiness." For many years the kinesthetic feeling of emptiness eluded me. In fact, I was troubled with the concept of nothingness—no God, no self—and with emptiness as an essential spiritual goal.

My conscious embodiment and aikido classes have always been places where I can work with life and spiritual issues. I take the time first to discuss and then create exercises to explore issues that are unclear or confusing. It is one thing to work with an idea as a concept or inner visualization either by ourselves or with a guide, but it is quite another to get up and interact with others in situations which represent threatening or confrontative encounters.

At a certain point in my life, I got the message that I needed to explore vulnerability, and so I took it onto the aikido mat. The experience of vulnerability made me very uncomfortable and I avoided it. Yet I sensed intuitively that it was important for me to explore and gain understanding of vulnerability. The first few times I intentionally evoked vulnerability, I experienced familiar fear reactions. But there were also glimmers of another aspect, a state of not-knowing, an innocence so profound that I sensed it had great potential.

If I was walking by myself, I could touch and embody the vulnerable state for two to three seconds. But when I was on the mat and a training partner punched at my belly, my capacity to hold this state was reduced to a half-second at best. I would find myself back in my familiar mode of doing: getting centered and blending with, or in some cases attacking the attacker. Nevertheless, I was impressed by the few times I was able to hold the state of not-knowing, and how that state totally changed both my experience and that of my partner. I knew I was on to something, but, in addition to my own habits, I was also up against a very deep and powerful cultural conditioning to protect myself and control the situation.

After a year or so, my capacity to extend the period that I could hold vulnerability and not-knowing developed. I began to notice that there were aspects of not-knowing I had not initially perceived. One very important aspect, what I call the "about-to-know" state, began to emerge. At last I understood what the Buddhists had meant by *shunyata*—emptiness. It was the pregnant space, the space or void from which all things come, the "about-to" phase of experience.

My favorite image of *shunyata* is that of an empty bowl with an open, full box of cereal poised above it. The bowl is *about to* be filled which is very different from an empty bowl in the cupboard. There is an intensity as the box hovers, its contents on the verge of falling into the bowl, while the empty bowl waits, a receptive place ready for conception.

Timing

As we attempt to penetrate the area of not-knowing, we need to start changing our concept of time. We want to be able to enter and elongate the space between thoughts—intervals as brief as fractions of a second. Anyone who has trained in sports, martial arts, or has practiced meditation understands that a part of a second can be a very long time. With training and discipline, we can begin to stretch these parts of a second and discover that there are whole worlds within them.

Consider the dynamics of professional baseball. As the batters stand over home plate watching the ball come toward them, they are dealing with less than a half of a second. Professional pitchers throw the ball at about ninety miles per hour; at this speed the ball takes four-tenths of a second to reach the catcher's mitt after leaving the pitcher's hand. If someone threw something at me at ninety miles per hour, I probably would not see it at all. Yet these batters are able to see the ball and make intuitive choices. They are able to elongate that four tenths of a second, see what they need to know, and take appropriate action. A whole world has opened up and all kinds of possibilities exist in a tiny fraction of a second.

Perhaps we can only hold our own about-to-know experience for a half-second before some kind of knowing arises. That half-second has tremendous potential. There is a phrase often used in *vipas-*

sana meditation, "choiceless awareness," which, in my experience, is another way of describing intuition. Once again, parts of a second become expanded so that the situation begins to open up and become spacious. In *vipassana* meditation, we observe the way our attention engages a thought process. We do this over and over and over again. On a ten-day retreat, meditators make these observations hour after hour, day after day. It is possible to arrive at the point where we can observe a thought about to happen. We can then observe ourselves choosing to think it or not. For me, it is like training to hit a ninety-mile-an-hour pitch and opening up time.

By surrendering to not-knowing, we can empty out our thoughts, wipe the slate clean, and create space for our intuition to come forth naturally and spontaneously. During not-knowing, our timing is tuned to the finesse of a millisecond. Timing has everything to do with satisfaction. When we eat, make love, exercise, or work at the right time, we feel quite satisfied. When our timing is off, it does not matter what we eat or how much we rest, satisfaction is not possible. If we can cultivate a spaciousness by developing our capacity for not-knowing, then our timing will become more accurate. We will be able to use intuitive timing, that is, timing where we no longer have to think, "Oh, I should do this now," but rather our doing arises naturally, spontaneously, just as a professional baseball player swings the bat.

Mystery

Emptiness and not-knowing are often referred to as the mystery. There is a story about a philosopher who goes to a Zen master for a teaching. The Zen master asks the philosopher if he would like tea and begins pouring. Soon the cup is filled and the tea begins to overflow onto the table and the floor. "What are you doing?" exclaims the philosopher in alarm. "You are like this cup," says the Zen master, "You come for information but you are completely full of ideas and beliefs. There is no room for anything more in your cup." Too often, we are like the philosopher. We cannot sense the mystery because we are so full of desire to achieve a result.

Recently, I was deeply moved by a conversation I had with a couple of friends. They have been married for seventeen or eighteen years and I was struck by the romantic quality I felt between them. When I asked about it, Rob said, "Kathy is fundamentally a mystery to me, so being around her is fascinating." Kathy acknowledged that Rob was also a mystery for her. What a great gift to give to the people we love: to allow them to be a mystery. I started practicing this with my children. When my son would come home from school, instead of greeting the boy I was so accustomed to, I took the attitude that I did not know who he was. I let go of my judgments and expectations and became interested in him. When I stopped thinking I knew all about the boy who would walk through the door, my son became a mystery to me. This has added a whole new dimension to our relationship and allows more softness and delight in our interactions.

What a wonderful gift we could give our loved ones, friends, students, clients, and teachers, if we could look at them with interest and a genuine curiosity. Instead, our perception of them is usually obscured by a huge bundle of knowledge and information we think we have about them. By expecting people to behave in a certain way, we tend to hold them to that way of being. For the most part we expect no surprises and we get none. We live in a world of projection, described by Plato as shadows on the wall of a cave. We mistake these shadows for the real thing that includes many textures with the intensity and poignancy of each moment. If we view the elements, situations, and people in our lives as unknown and mysterious, anything is possible.

Strength of Spirit

Looking at the world with interest, openness, and curiosity may sound like a wonderful idea, but the actual *doing* of it is based on strength: the strength of spirit, which develops our concentration through discipline and practice. Strength of spirit enables us to keep our heart soft while we tolerate and accept the intensity of feelings and sensations. We can remember Musashi's statement, "The purpose of today's training is to defeat yesterday's understanding." We must not rest on the laurels of yesterday's memory, but engage each moment with fresh interest and curiosity. By finding a way to stabilize and return to the present, just here and just now, we set the stage for not-knowing, a place in which intuition may arise. We develop a simple straightforward sense of self through basic practice by using the elements of breath, awareness of our field, and sensations of gravity. This sense of self is our base, our reference point or platform from which we can leap into the pool of not-knowing. To develop strength of spirit, we use basic practice and train every day using courage, humor, and patience to bring our attention back to the moment. Then we can learn to focus, even for a fraction of a second, into the cracks of not-knowing and expand our sense of mystery as a real and valid part of our lives.

Chapter Eight

Intuition

Would existence without personal friends be to you a blank?
Then the time will come when you will be solitary, left with-
out sympathy; but this seeming vacuum is already filled with
divine love.

Mary Baker Eddy

Intuition is a knowing that arises spontaneously in our being. This knowing appears as an insight with accompanying sensations that are the basis of bodily intuition. Intuition literally means being taught from within. As young children most of us are embodied and have access to our intuition. Children usually know how they feel and how their parents feel. Children, so-called "primitive peoples," and animals are much more sensitive than most civilized adults and can perceive the deep feelings and intentions that exist under a surface attitude.

When a child responds in a way that seems contrary to what an adult is expressing, the child may be regarded as rude or nasty. All too often, adults are not aware of all that exists under their surface expression or that they are trying to hide their true feelings. Young children can sense those true feelings and intentions until they are trained not to feel what is really going on.

Children growing up in our "civilized" culture tend to have their intuition suppressed. Biological development may have something to do with this, but there is a clearer correlation in our socialization experience. There seems to be a cultural standard that children should not be able to see into the adult inner life. The message to children is: "What you see and feel is not true. It is just your imagination." Sometimes subtle and sometimes not, these messages come from adults, older children, and most significantly parents. For instance, a young child senses some discomfort and asks the mother, "What's wrong?" The mother, who may feel embarrassed or is trying to "protect" her child, replies, "Nothing." In fact, something *is* wrong and the mother is trying to keep that something from the child. Rather than be in opposition to their parents, children will almost always suppress their intuition. We are taught that we should not trust our intuitive selves or what we sense and feel.

Working from a Stable Base

We need to have enough stability in order to differentiate our projections from our impressions. An impression is information that comes to us through our intuitive self. A projection is an impression that becomes distorted by our fears and/or desires. Our projections are often habitualized, and because there is usually some truth in our distorted perceptions, we assume we have the correct information. In fact we are the worst kind of right—"sort of right." We have some correct information and some distorted information. The information has its original intuitive feel, but we lack the clarity to see the difference between it and our own stuff. This is dangerous because the advice we give, or the actions we take, are distorted by our reactive projections. The goal of intuition training is to be able to separate our projections from our intuitive voice.

Psychics have either found a way to separate their own biases from the information, or they have retained the intuitive abilities of their youth so the information they receive is not distorted. Chögyam Trungpa defines wisdom this way: "One intuitively knows everything already; it is independent of amassing information." This knowing can be divided into three categories: clairvoyance or "clearseeing"—or knowing that comes from visual images or symbols; clairaudience or "clearhearing"—knowing that comes from an inner voice or words of some kind; and clairsentience or "clearfeeling"—knowing that comes through sensations or feelings in the body.

I believe that everyone has complete intuitive capabilities. Some people can easily access intuitive knowing. They have usually developed one sense over the others: we often hear psychics referred to as clairvoyant. For others, this knowledge lies below thick layers of fear and desire and takes the form of resistance or confusion. Knowing something about the structure of our fears and desires helps us penetrate through the layers of resistance and confusion. If we have the courage to examine ourselves, we can begin to understand and face our intuitive impressions. Conscious embodiment gives us a way to reconnect with our sensations, making it possible to find the path to the still space from which intuitive impressions arise.

Not-Knowing: The Doorway

When we use basic practice to center ourselves, we enter into a moment of stability which is soft and open. This is a good moment to ask for the intuitive knowledge we seek. Centering "clears the slate" and allows us to be open and empty, like a cup waiting to be filled. In this state of not-knowing, intuition can arise. We are like a cup waiting to be filled. It is a moment of tremendous intimacy: there is no agenda and no boundary. The wisdom of our intuition enters, and we see, hear, or feel the answer.

Not-knowing has to do with depth, space, and stillness. Depth comes from confidence and confidence is built from experience, which comes from the practice of training our attention. The more we develop ourselves, the more we can tolerate the sensation of the present. To be in the present, with no past or no future, no agenda of any kind, is a very intense experience. Most of us are not able to tolerate the present for very long and after a few minutes or seconds, we shift to the past or the future.

When we can begin to tolerate the present, we start to experience space. Since we are not crowded with thoughts of the past or the future, the present becomes very spacious. Once we can hold a sense of space—in front of us, behind us, to the left and right, above and below—we can begin to work with the element of stillness. Stillness is the "about-to" place. When we are poised, completely present, and ready, we are at the entrance to not-knowing or "don't-know mind," the place where intuition and the creative impulse spring forth.

By strengthening our ability to center through basic practice, we can quiet ourselves, stabilize, and open to intuition. We need to build our tolerance so that the energy and sensations we receive can be correctly interpreted. If we become ungrounded, it is easy to distort the message.

A strong deep sense of center allows us to tolerate the not-knowing as well as the knowing. Not-knowing is the creative, receptive state from which everything is born. There is a lot of fear associated with not-knowing since most of us got an "F" for not knowing the "correct" answer to something. This fear of not-knowing creates a very tight or claustrophobic situation internally.

Through practice and training, we can learn to tolerate and even enjoy the open, pregnant space of not-knowing. We are patient and can wait for the spontaneous appearance of our intuition. Instead of panicky feelings associated with confusion, we can allow ourselves to experience a relaxed, open feeling. There are no agendas or opinions. We have no idea of what we will see, hear, or feel.

Creating Manageable Pieces for the Process

Intuitive impressions can be overwhelming and when we are overwhelmed, we get off center and distort the message. By learning to ask ourselves questions that focus on separate pieces of the situation, we get manageable and pertinent bits of information. We can use the triad of questions introduced in Chapter Six: "Where is the power or strength in the situation?" "Where is the weakness or least amount of energy?" And, "What is the next step or what is needed?" In actuality, there are very few things that we need to know in order to act skillfully and compassionately. Sometimes even one question can be enough to give us the information we need.

In order to ready myself to ask the questions, I bring myself to center using basic practice. Once my attention has been collected within myself, I open my energy field, expand my awareness, and consider the person or situation with a question. I ask myself the question, "Where is the power?" Then, I have to be willing genuinely to not know. I have to be soft and wait. When the impression arises either as a voice, feeling, or visual image, I accept it exactly as it is. If I want clarification, I center again, ask again, and wait with a genuine feeling that I do not know what the message is going to be. This sequence is repeated for each question, taking time to come back to myself and center each time. The knowledge we access with these questions allows us to act skillfully and compassionately in the next moment.

It is important to realize that we do not need more than this intuitive information. To seek more is simply being "greedy" and comes from a place of insecurity. We would like to assure our position and fix things so that we feel safe. This way of being is not our true path and we have to have courage and discipline to move away from grasping after more than we need. With basic practice we can learn to come back to center and to the presence of breath, balance, and gravity. Coming back to center is not trying to assure the future of anything. This is the powerful spiritual practice of being here, right in the moment—the sensations of now.

The intelligence of this centered state surfaces spontaneously and intuitively. There are instances in all our lives when we have been able to act brilliantly even without the presence of our cognitive understanding, only realizing afterward that we functioned at the level of wisdom.

Interpreting

We can interact with intuitive energies in many ways, including the intellectual, physical, and other dimensions. These preexisting agendas draw us toward a certain style of interaction with the energy. Our interpretation of the situation is influenced by the way we choose to interact with the energy.

The intellectual approach is when we seek information that fits into a previously established concept. We know what we are trying to get information about, but we do not know what the information is. The process of asking the three questions falls into this category. With this approach, we have a mental agenda: we are interested in finding out a specific thing about a certain situation. When we ask the questions about power, weakness, and the next step, we receive an "intellectual knowing." We engage our minds to ask the questions even though the "answers" we receive may be feelings, images, words, or sounds.

During physical activities, we are after a kinesthetic or "feeling knowing." In body-oriented situations like aikido or sports, we do not have time to ask a mental question. By the time we have asked the question, it is too late. In fact, we want to keep the intellect out of it altogether and allow our energy field to respond automatically. In order to suspend thinking, we occupy our attention with basic practice. We concentrate on the movement of our breath, the balance and perimeter of our field, and gravity and our receptivity to the earth. When we focus in this way, our system responds automatically, sometimes brilliantly. Of course, there are learning periods during which we must teach ourselves the moves, such as when we learn to drive a car. In the beginning, we have to think to use the turn signal or to put the car into gear, but after a short while our bodies do them automatically—we no longer have to think about these things. We allow the wisdom of intuition to flow through us when we focus on basic practice and stay in the present moment.

Shamans and healers use the intuitive process in a different way. Sometimes they seek to be drawn into another dimension rather than pulling information from it. These are the dimensions of spirits, archetypal and mythological energies, and otherworldly beings. To function in these realms, we must be willing to die, in both a metaphorical and even a literal sense. We must be able to completely abandon our concepts of real and unreal, bad and good, life and death. We must enter these dimensions as a warrior, without looking back or trying to compare, relate, or hold onto anything. In these worlds, energies manifest and interact as beings. Wisdom arises when we courageously face and interact with the manifestations of our fears and desires. Ironically, it sometimes takes more courage to interact with manifestations of our beauty and strength.

Nonverbal Communication

Every living thing reflects an intelligence that the human intellect cannot index or adequately explain and therefore cannot be taught from an external source.
> —J. Allen Boone

Nonverbal communication can involve intuition. Its intuitive quality lies in the sometimes illogical interactions we have with animals, nature, and infants. Our actions may seem illogical in many situations because our logic would tell us that it would be dangerous to do what we were doing, like the time I snuck into the corral and stole a ride on the "dangerous stallion." In that case, my intuition—my sense that I would not be hurt—overrode the logical part that said, "You might be hurt."

The logical side of nonverbal communication with animals is reflected in training a dog or horse. For instance, animal trainers use a series of repetitions to train the animal to respond to a look or gesture. This is not particularly intuitive or creative. Using these training techniques, if I want to train a dog to lie down, I might snap my fingers and point to the ground where the dog is standing. At first, I might have to press the dog physically into lying position. When I snap my fingers and point and the dog does lie down, I give the reward of a pat and a kind word. When the dog does not lie down when I give the nonverbal command, I again physically press the dog into the down position. After hundreds or thousands of repetitions, I can snap my fingers, point to the ground and the dog will lie down. After being trained to the gesture, the dog will usually lie down when people other than the trainer give the nonverbal command by snapping their fingers and pointing down.

Another form of nonverbal communication occurs if we are not trying to train an animal to do something in particular, but are instead open to just being with the animal in the moment. When we are not trying to dominate the animal, the animal may initiate the interaction. I am particularly fond of a friend's dog. One day I was visiting my friend and as we were talking, her dog approached and looked at me. I looked back for a minute and found myself saying, "So you want to go for a walk. Okay, let's go." That day we had a lovely walk together. There are beautiful moments that can be shared with animals if we can quiet down enough and allow ourselves to connect with them. It is important to keep in mind that the basis of intuition is not-knowing, so that spontaneous, creative ideas, insights, or actions come from being open and awake while not-thinking, from the subconscious, or from whatever you want to call that place of mystery.

When Robert Frost wrote his famous poem, "The Road Less Taken," about two divergent paths, one road more often traveled than the other, he used both logic and intuition. Frost used his logic to imagine the adventures each road might hold because of the way it looked. His intuition came forward in his decision-making process because there was really no way to know for sure what either road would bring. His sense was that both roads were equally appealing in different ways. His final decision to take "the one less travelled by" was an intuitive choice because both roads were unknown to him.

Anytime I go out into nature, I use both rational logic and intuition. Using my logic means that I dress sensibly, take water, and consider other physical and safety needs. With my intuition I open myself to the mystery and allow something to arise, either from nature, where I might see or feel something special, or from myself as I am drawn to a particular place where suddenly I grasp a new understanding.

We could think of nonverbal communication as a radar system. We send out vibrations that bounce off other people and come back to us with information, both about the other person and ourselves. These vibes can be carried in the subtleties of our posture and gestures or they may be as invisible as the sound waves that carry radio transmissions.

Underlying messages of fear, love, resentment, and admiration are picked up through our internal radar systems. Intuitives can know deep feelings and read intentions that exist under a surface attitude. Since many of us are not completely aware of what exists under our own surface attitude, we are sometimes surprised when children or animals respond in a way that seems contrary to what we are saying or how we are acting. For example, we may act in a way that is sweet and polite, but deep inside we feel resentful. When children or animals respond to the resentment, we may become angry and judgmental, thinking that they are rude or nasty.

As lovers, whether our love is with nature, art, or another being, we create an automatic, intuitive bond. We know or sense what is beyond words. During the moments when we feel this profound connection, we know we belong in the universe. We no longer have the sense of being expelled from the garden, of being outcasts trying to reason and earn our way back. When we love, we are no longer in the realm of good and bad, right and wrong; we are linked with the pulse of the universe. When we are aware of our connection to the universe, nothing is hidden. Pain and pleasure dance as brother and sister, both necessary parts of the whole. Our systems know where and when to move or be still. This amazing gift is always there inside us. If we can collect and focus ourselves within, enter the sanctuary of not-knowing, and have the courage to wait; then we can be filled and we will be able to hear, see, and/or feel the essential nature of things.

Part III

Wisdom Arising—
Ways Our Soma
Is Organized

Chapter Nine

The Energetic Field

*There is a basic state of existence that is fundamentally good
and that we can rely on. There is room to relax, room to open
ourselves up. We can make friends with ourselves and others.*

Chögyam Trungpa

Each of us is immersed in an energetic field which can be intuitively sensed and can also be measured either as heat or subtle electromagnetic energy. Intuitively, we experience our field as a kind of atmosphere or fragrance that surrounds us. Our field has a shape or dimension which we can affect or alter. When we become aware of the energetic field around us, we can be more present and know that it is part of the sensation of being. The shape of our energetic field is flexible and will expand or contract according to our situation and mood. For example, when we are happy, excited, or interested, our field tends to expand; when we are afraid or depressed, it tends to contract. When the size of our field changes, the message we send to the external world also changes.

In class I say, "Imagine your field as a shape. Does a particular shape immediately come to mind?" The three shapes that O Sensei used were a circle, a square, and a triangle. The circle is about relationship: with a circle we can either include or exclude others. The square conveys groundedness: being stable, steadfast, and solid. The triangle implies mobilization: cutting through, moving forward, or *irimi*, which means to enter, or move in. I discuss *irimi* in detail in Chapter Twelve.

I often ask, "What size and shape is your field?" Usually, we are quite frontal, focusing more attention or energy on the front of ourselves than on the back. By focusing our attention, imagination, and breath, we can practice affecting our field by giving it a particular size and shape.

In addition to having a shape, energetic fields also have a texture. A smooth quality will keep people or things from clinging or sticking onto us because they slide right off. Workaholics often have a slick texture to their field. Some people have an almost "velcro"-like quality to their fields: everything clings onto them. They try to move forward while dragging along a lot of extraneous responsibility. People with this sticky texture in their energy field can feel exhausted and have difficulty in getting moving, like a depressed person. Again by using our attention, imagination, and breath, we can practice making different shapes and then giving textures to our energy field. We can switch back and forth from smooth and penetrating to soft and absorbing, experiencing the difference between the them.

To establish the perimeter of my field, I ask myself the question, "Is the front of my field equal to the back?" and wait for the sensations that follow the question. Then I become interested in and ask about the left and right sides of my field, again waiting to see if there is any shift or change. Next, I ask and sense above and below me. I let my interest lead my awareness, waiting to see if there is any sense of expansion or contraction. I can choose to affect my field. By using my quality, I can change my mood, cheer myself up, or bring myself to stillness. Introducing the notion that I am about to see, hear, or feel some insight alters the shape of my field and my relationship to myself and others.

Our field communicates a particular message to the outside world. For example, it can say: "come closer" or "don't get so close." Generally, I find that what people say verbally and what they communicate through their field are not always in agreement. This disparity creates confusion and stress in relationships. The other person has to decide if they are going to relate to what we are saying verbally or to what our field is expressing.

Our field is affected as well by the intensity and focus of our glance. In his memoirs, O Sensei spoke about this:

> Don't look at the opponent's eyes, or your mind will be drawn into his eyes. Don't look into his sword or you will be slain with his sword. Don't look at him or your spirit will be distracted. True *Budo* is the cultivation of attraction ... that is, we draw him into ourselves.

Clearly, O Sensei is talking about a particular kind of interaction and I am not suggesting that this is the only way to use our glance or to affect our field. However, I am suggesting that we can develop some discipline about the way our energy travels to and from our field.

Our eyes are the gates to a tremendous amount of energy or *ki.* Here in the West we are often unconscious of the degree to which this energy can affect a given situation. We think we are just looking, while in reality we are focusing a tremendous amount of energy towards the object of our gaze. There is a nonreceptivity about most looking because the energy flows outward. In some situations a gaze can be so strong it feels almost like a blow.

Asian cultures, among others, are very conscious of the energy and intensity in the gaze. A student once told me about being in China. She had been there off and on for over two years and was not completely new to the culture. She said she would be riding her bicycle along and see a family cooking something by the side of the road. As she would look to see what they were doing, they would look up startled and fearful as if she had yelled or struck at them. She told me that even after two years, her glaze was still so invasive to many of the Chinese people that it produced this fearful, negative reaction.

People of Asian cultures know much more about containment than we do in the West. On the other hand, Westerners know much more about expression than many Eastern people. It seems to me that both cultures can learn from each other. However, at this time, we are concerned with the issue of awareness of our energy and how we are using it. Our gaze has a lot to do with the size, shape, and texture of our field. Attraction has a lot to do with the quality of receptivity in the glance.

"Discipline is freedom," I often say. When we practice and embody different ways of organizing the flow of our energy, we encourage our intuition to guide us—spontaneously organizing how we respond to a given situation. We can arrest our gaze and stabilize our field. We can draw energy toward or away from us with the texture of our field. By becoming aware of the shape of our field, knowing what we want to communicate, and recognizing the relationship between our gaze and our energetic field, we can increase our capacity for flexibility and unification.

Shaping Our Field: Triangle, Square, and Circle

At this level of our practice, we are not just letting things unfold, we are training our being in conscious embodiment. We can begin with a particular concept in our mind—say that of mobilizing ourselves and cutting through a problem. Then we can practice organizing our field into a triangle or wedge shape. We feel our texture as smooth and we focus our awareness on what we want to move toward. We pay attention to the smooth, penetrating quality of the field. Our muscles are soft and our concentration is firm. Through the practice of focusing our field, we gain an alternative way of dealing with a problem or coping when we are emotionally overwhelmed.

Ideally, we have great depth or a large field which can handle or accept the full range of emotions from dark to light without wanting to change something or have it be another way. As we develop a greater tolerance for the elements of the present moment, we strengthen both body and spirit, allowing the rich and mysterious shades of our feelings and emotions to arise, including happiness, sadness, pleasure, and pain.

What is it about the square that implies a stable and settled feeling? When I think about it, a square is not a shape that I am inclined to throw. I do not think of squares hurtling through space. I think of a square as staying put. When we say things are "squared away," it implies a steady, stable situation. When two people become deadlocked in challenging each other for space, they are said to be "squared off." When they come into agreement, they are said to be "square with" each other.

Most of us literally live in either squares or rectangles. These shapes are associated with our notion of "home," which usually conjures up the feeling of a secure, stable space. How about an A-frame or a dome? I have spent a little time in both of these alternative dwellings and they have a very different feel from the square shape of our usual housing. There is a sense of loft or lightness about the A-frame and the dome; they are not so earthbound.

The easiest way to begin sensing our field as a square is to use the room we are in as the perimeter. We then expand our field to fill the room so it becomes an expanded square shape. Imagine what it would be like if we were to hold this "square" feeling and go through an entire day with the awareness that we had this size and shape exuding from us. I am sure that the quality of some of our encounters would be different than usual.

What would be some of the advantages of this energy? What would be some of the disadvantages? Provided that we are willing to concentrate our attention in order to develop a square energy field, we can ask if there is anything useful in this shape and feeling that could benefit us. Many houses are square with a triangular shape on top. The bottom walls and foundation have a solid "squared off" sense and the roof or top has a sense of loft or upward movement. Many churches have an exaggerated sense of movement toward heaven because of their steeples or spires. What is it like to sense ourselves as stable on the bottom, our legs and hips solid, while at the same time, extending and lifting upward with our spine and head?

O Sensei spoke about "heaven and earth." In an aikido technique called *tenshi nage*, or the "heaven-and-earth throw," we extend downward and upward simultaneously. The idea is to split our attacker's attention between heaven and earth. One hand draws the attacker downward, while the other hand draws the attacker upward. This is one example of a square interacting with a triangle.

Practicing Being Both Positive and Receptive

Positive/Receptive is an exercise which encourages flexibility and wholeness. The concept that the universe is expanding simultaneously in all directions can be applied to positive/receptive. Every situation has potential for balance and wholeness. If, for example, when we are walking backward and we can feel that we are moving into or toward something, we no longer have to associate backward with "moving away" from something. Moving backward is not a negative experience: we have not failed. We are simply moving and our willingness to make contact is a positive outflow with no implication of loss whatsoever.

In order to be more comfortable moving backward, we need to contact and awaken the backs of our bodies and energy fields. When we can appreciate our backsides, we can trust them to lead us backward. Moving backwards then becomes a positive experience, a movement toward what is behind us. To develop our ability to move backward, I often suggest going to a track and walking backward for a mile or so. Usually after about a half mile, the back begins to "wake up." We begin to feel or sense a kind of presence and intelligence in our backfield. Walking backward then becomes similar to riding on a train facing the caboose, we can relax and watch the scenery move away from us.

Once we are more familiar, confident, and relaxed while moving backward, we can open ourselves and become interested in what is there. Instead of feeling panicky and claustrophobic about moving backward, we can welcome moving, soften a bit, and provide enough space for our intuition and proper timing to arise. When this occurs, we automatically function more skillfully, more compassionately. When the time is right, we can turn any situation around. And then, without aggression or effort, we are walking forward.

Now, as we move forward, we can examine the balance of power. First, we must drop any idea that forward is better. As long as we only want to move forward and do not want to move backward, we are setting ourselves up to suffer and be unhappy. Desire and aversion create conflict. Our inner conflict is what makes us so unhappy. Moving forward is simply a direction, not any better than moving backward, sideways, up, or down. When we move forward, we let ourselves be relaxed and open. We need to be receptive to what we are moving toward and welcome it while we are moving toward it. If we remember to sense the back of our fields as we move forward, we can experience a greater sense of wholeness.

Practice walking backward and forward. Switch off. First walk backward and then walk forward. Keep switching back and forth until both directions begin to feel the same. Once they start to feel the same, we can test ourselves with a partner. During this exercise in class I say, "Notice how, as soon as you engage in relationship with another, things change. Perhaps it is harder to keep your awareness of the back and front of your field, or the relaxed spaciousness you had when you were moving by yourself. That's fine. Now you have something to work for."

This exercise gives us a sense of how much concentration, confidence, and connection to ourselves we need to develop in order to stay whole and balanced in relationship to others. When we can start to face the truth, we realize how easily we are thrown off and lose our sense of self when someone comes toward us or moves away from us. This positive/receptive exercise can give us more incentive to apply basic practice in our lives. With basic practice, we exercise our ability to develop a strong connection to ourselves in the present moment, and this connection allows our wisdom and intuition to arise and guide us.

Chapter Ten

Attentional States

As a well-trained horse needs no whip, a well-trained mind needs no prodding from the world to be good. Be like a well-trained horse, swift and spirited, and go beyond sorrow through faith, meditation, and energetic practice of the dharma.

Buddha

There are three functional attentional states: dropped, open, and blended. Each of the attentional states can be used for different purposes. Dropped attention is focused on the self, open attention includes others, while blended attention has no reference point yet we are simultaneously ourselves and the other.

Being open all of the time is not always the most skillful way of being. Sometimes it is more skillful just to deal with ourselves and not necessarily include everyone around us and the surrounding environment. There are times when it is essential to come back to just ourselves for a moment. Blended attention is the most difficult to attain and cannot be achieved through trying. All three states have advantages and disadvantages.

Dropped Attention

Dropped attention is the state that we experience in basic practice. It is the starting point, the place where we collect and focus ourselves within. Dropped attention is the practice of developing a self to be true to and to come back to, as well as a state from which we relate to others. All attentional states have fallen sides, and dropped attention can serve to contract us or pull us away from others rather than help us to collect and gather ourselves.

A phenomenon frequently occurs when people come down and into their bodies for the first time: they feel stable, soft, and present, yet they will begin to cry or experience an intense feeling of sadness. When someone experiences a sudden stability and softness, why might he or she also become sad? A Persian word, *durie*, translated as "homesickness" or "longing," describes this sad sensation. *Durie* implies a longing or homesickness for the beloved, a yearning for unity. We cannot experience homesickness unless we are aware of the separation. As we begin to connect with ourselves, the realization of how far away we have been from ourselves becomes apparent, and with this realization comes the sadness and the longing to connect with ourselves, the beloved within.

Years ago I had a very powerful experience with a Tibetan lama. I went to see him to discuss my sense of aloneness and abandonment issues that have been with me throughout my life. I had been thinking of my experience of these feelings as a fallen side to my spirituality. I thought that if I had true spirituality, if my spirituality were strong enough, I would not feel so alone or abandoned. The lama told me, "No, you are alone. You are born alone and you die alone. You are absolutely right." With these words an incredible relief flooded me. I felt that now I could begin to make genuine connection. I no longer tried to make connection in order to get away from this "bad" thing, the uncomfortable feeling of being alone. The lama verified my state as an acceptable human condition as he said, "Both are true. You are completely alone and you are intrinsically connected to all other beings. You are not a bad person and it is not a lack of spirituality that you are experiencing. When you die, you die alone." He had shown me that both aloneness and connectedness are part of spiritual practice. Both are true and necessary.

And, so it is in dropped attention—we are alone. It is the "getting it together with ourselves." In class I often say, "It's you and you." Open attention represents the connected aspect to living. It is absolutely imperative that we tolerate both open and dropped states. We may have a preference for one or the other, but we need to be able to function skillfully in both states. We need to be able to accept and function in our experience of being alone, as well as to accept and function in our experience of connectedness with all things.

Open Attention

Open attention is what I call the "contemporary state," a state of "self and included others." Open attention is the state we are in during most of our interactions with people. Moving from dropped attention, where we have gathered energy and focused our attention to a deep place, we can expand to include the surrounding situation. To do so, it is necessary to expand in all directions—to the back, front, left, right, above and below—so that we can maintain balance and stay in our own working center with open attention. Our energy field becomes more like a sphere or circle.

To visualize open attention, think of the structure of an atom as drawn in a beginning-level science book, the nucleus in the center with the electrons spinning around it. In class I suggest, "Imagine you are the the nucleus of an atom and the people around you are the electrons." Our job as a nucleus is to stabilize or hold the space for those inside our field. When we work with our field in this way, it becomes large enough to include the other people and some space around them.

In working with the size of my field and open attention, I may ask myself, "How deep do I need to be? And, how wide do I need to be to hold the space for those inside my field?" It is important to remember that we are stabilizing the space or environment, *not* trying to change the people in it. It is also important to keep sensing the width and depth of the space so we can steady the field and allow natural creative movement to take place without grasping or resisting any part of the situation.

Two people holding space for each other can allow powerful feelings to flow without either becoming off-center. If both people can hold the space, above, below, and all around as intensely as the feelings flowing from their hearts, then they can love in a balanced and powerful way. Holding the space allows each person to be the way he or she is without trying to make him or her different.

To begin sensing our energy field, we can first apply our imagination in a "let's pretend" manner. As we become more accustomed feeling our field, we no longer have to apply our imagination in this manner because we will automatically sense the size of the field necessary to hold the energy of the situation. Since we tend to put most of our attention on those things in front of us, we have to be sure to think about the space behind us as well as the space to the sides, above, and below us.

Open attention is very powerful—we have accepted others completely and made space for their entire range of behavior without trying to change them. This is what the Buddhists mean by compassion. In order to do this, we must have a tremendous amount of ground. We not only ground ourselves, but we hold the space for others inside our field so we can tolerate their energy without losing our center. Our field becomes a foundation or root system that can hold their emotional and psychic weight.

One of the wonderful side effects of open attention is that when others are fully accepted, the other person's capacity to resist or go against is diminished. The magnetic situation that we spoke about earlier tends to draw or align their energy toward an experience of softness and ground. It is important to be clear that changing them is *not* our goal.

When we center and open our attention in order to develop ourselves, others tend to be drawn into our quiet state. If we are trying to change others rather than accepting them as they are, our attention has a secondary agenda and is no longer unified. When our attention is split in this way, it can result in numerous problems. More details of split attentional states are discussed in Chapter Eleven.

The state of open attention has tremendous integrity. We are not trying to get anybody to do anything; we include the situation just as it is. If we are open and find that the energy we are attempting to include is too strong, then we adjust—we must return to dropped attention so our attention will not be split. Again, it is the split that can cause us to ellipt or be drawn into the other person's space. When part of us is drawn into the other person's space, our boundaries begin to destabilize and we experience conflict of some sort which is frequently focused on the other person.

A student of conscious embodiment recounts a story about shifting between dropped and open attention:

> My best friend and I got together to discuss the changing nature of our friendship. It was an awkward and uncomfortable time for both of us. My main issue in our relationship was that I had always allowed her needs to take precedence. I was so involved with her and her needs that I had forgotten that I had any.
>
> When I realized I did in fact have needs, I became resentful. As we talked I found myself leaning forward so much, both physically and emotionally, to meet her that I lost myself. When I realized I had ellipted onto her, I would return to dropped attention and become aware of my breath. After I reestablished a relationship with myself, I could expand my field to include her again using open attention.
>
> Then there were times when I was aware that my attention was becoming so dropped that I was excluding her and not hearing what she had to say.
>
> Thus, I experienced the downside of both dropped and open attention. My tendency has always been toward co-dependence, so this is not an easy practice for me to follow. But, during this meeting with my friend, I was encouraged and felt that being interested in myself does not have to exclude the other person and can, in fact, be a much more authentic way of being.
>
> This was an important lesson for me: to know that in coming back to myself, I am benefiting both myself and the other person much more than if I give myself up to her.
>
> —Sharon

Ellipted Attention

The fallen side of open attention is what I call "ellipted attention," because we have unevenly projected our energy field onto another person or situation. Like an ellipse we have two centers compared to our balanced circle which only has one center. In the state of ellipted attention, we are split between our center and the other person's center. Ellipted attention is useful to our neurosis in that it distracts us from having to feel fully or relate to ourselves. Codependency is another term for ellipted attention. The worst-case scenario is when we can only feel ourselves in terms of the other person. Rather than opening and including someone else in our field, our awareness shifts out onto the other person and the other person becomes more interesting to us than we are to ourselves. In this state we are no longer in our working center. We are either in between our center and someone else's center, or again, in the worst case, we have merged with the other person and are lost completely.

Ellipted attention is a very dangerous state. Take the image of a record on a turntable: if you put a penny on the outer edge of the record and start the turntable, the penny will be flung off. However, when you place the penny at the center of the record, it can tolerate a lot more speed and stay on the record. Our attention is the same way: if my attention has moved outside of my center and is either on the edge of my field or placed upon someone else, I will be very vulnerable to whatever that person does. When the other person moves around or acts inconsistently, I will be flung off my center. If I can keep my awareness in my own working center and expand to include the other person, it is easier for me to tolerate the fluctuations in both of us.

In Western culture, there is a strong tendency toward ellipted attention. When others become more interesting, either positively or negatively, we tend to lose ourselves and our center of awareness becomes focused on them. In this ellipted state, whatever the other person does is going to affect us. If we can recognize this, we can use our practice of dropped attention to bring us back to our own center. Then we can expand our field in a spherical way to include the other person while we are still in our own working center. With training we begin to develop a self to come back to. When we notice that another person has become more interesting or compelling than our sense of ourselves, it is important to make a shift. If we care about and want to help the other person, we can do so in a more balanced way when we come back to ourselves first. I believe the greatest service we can do anyone on the planet is to get ourselves together. In my opinion, this is the most generous thing we can do. Ellipted attention is very seductive so we must really be conscious when we are in open attention.

There are more subtle forms of ellipted behavior. With partial shifts, our attention is somewhat on ourselves and somewhat on the other. This split in our attention is more difficult to identify because we are only noticing one part of ourselves. This interesting phenomenon is the topic of Chapter Eleven.

Another student tells a story of using a dropped versus an ellipted attentional state during a work crisis:

> I work as a counselor at a youth center for severely emotionally-disturbed adolescents. It is both challenging and rewarding to work in this environment. And sometimes it becomes very stressful. These battered and abused children continue to act out their violence on those around them. When all those around me are very chaotic and out of control, I now use dropped attention as a method of centering on myself.
>
> Recently after I had set some limits with one of the teenagers, she started yelling in my face and I remembered to practice dropped attention. I was able to focus on my breath and the space around me rather than enter into a power struggle with this very upset young lady. Almost immediately I felt a shift in my stance and posture. This shift must have been sensed by the youth because she left my area and began to calm down.
>
> I also found that my awareness while this girl was yelling at me took on a different perspective. I became interested in looking at how she was viewing this situation rather than trying to confront or lecture her as I had done in previous circumstances. I have discovered that I am one of those who usually maintains ellipted attention rather than being with myself in dropped attention.
>
> I am learning that it is best to focus on myself first and foremost, and then go to an open stance after I am well grounded in my own space because I can better keep my center and act in a more balanced manner.
>
> —Roseann

Blended Attention

A third attentional state, blended attention, is very difficult to maintain. I describe it as a state that has no reference point in which we are simultaneously self and other. We sometimes experience blended attention during a crisis, in lovemaking, maybe even while driving, or during those moments in an athletic activity when we can do no wrong. Blended attention is the state where we are expanded throughout the situation, but we are not asleep or spaced out.

In aikido the blend is what dissolves the conflict. When we blend, we *go with* the energy or direction of the attack. From a mental standpoint, the head center, we "see the world from the attacker's point of view." The heart center tends to feel what our partner is feeling. The *hara*, or belly, knows how and where the body will move. When all three centers make contact with those of our partner, we have the sense that we have disappeared. We become so like the person who has attacked us that there is no one to attack. Aggression is based on duality. In class I explain, "There has to be two, both you and me. If I see you as different from me, I can attack you. On the other hand, if you are similar to me, you are more difficult to attack." By making a complete blend, we do just this. It is also referred to as neutralizing the attack.

When discussing attentional-states, blended attention is the hardest one to define. And, in experiencing the sensations of each state, blended attention is the hardest one to maintain. Blended attention is difficult to hold because when we do experience it, as soon as we say, "That's it," we lose it. Once we have said "it," we have created a reference point and the blended state is gone. Blended attention is an incredibly powerful state. The great mystics are able to stay in this blended state for long periods of time and tolerate it skillfully because they have trained the reference point, also known as the ego, to dissolve while they maintain awareness. Usually when we enter blended attention, we very quickly catapult ourselves out of it. Then we can only refer to blended attention in the past, saying, "What was that?" or, "That was it!"

The *Tao Te Ching* describes blended attention as "no color, no taste." Blended attention is often described as what it is not, because the concepts of language are not adequate to talk about it. The fallen side of blended attention is that as soon as we enter it, it is so powerful that it knocks us out of it.

There is an important distinction between blending and merging: when we are blending, we retain a sense of self so that we can easily and quickly shift back to that self as opposed to merging when we can lose ourselves in the other person. When we blend, we do not get lost in our partner nor do we do get confused about who we are. When we merge with someone, we tend to dissolve and confuse our identity with them as in ellipted attention. For some people, this habit is so strong that they do not have any sense of themselves. They can only feel themselves through other people, "self as other," as Helen Palmer calls it. Clearly this is a problematic view. If our well-being is based on "other," we are sure to suffer and be unhappy.

However, blending and merging both share a momentary experience of empathy like "standing in the other person's shoes." The difference between the two lies in our ability to recognize that we are different from the other person, and that we have a sense of self or autonomy. This sense of self needs to be intact, along with the discipline actually to shift back to ourselves.

A very interesting thing happens when we shift to blended attention—it seems to magnetically draw the energy of others or the attacker into the state of the blender. At this point we can move from the blend to redirecting the energy. The osmotic quality of energetic "follow-the-leader" allows this change to happen. Now, the one who is blending needs inspiration and vision—the qualities of leadership which direct the form of the change.

Training Attentional States

As always, if we want to develop, we must practice. Repetition develops the capacity to embody or manifest these energetic states of being. We need to exercise the "muscle of attention," so our energy can follow and reorganize itself in a different pattern.

To train our attentional states, we begin with dropped attention in basic practice. Then we focus on our breathing, balance, gravity, and adding our quality. Once we have established ourselves through sensation, we begin to expand in all directions. We can include other people or just expand by ourselves in a room. We use our breath and our imagination to stabilize the perimeter of our energy field while we maintain our sense of it. If we find it difficult to focus on ourselves as center, we can focus on the perimeter because it will imply the center. Now our experience of ourself is expanded and spacious. We have room for people or things inside our space.

We also need to develop enough depth or groundedness to accept and tolerate the energy of the people or things within our field. If we feel spacy, distracted, or uncomfortable, we can stay with it a few more seconds and then shift our attention back to dropped attention. We will feel a change in the sensation now that our attention is focused closer in. Remember, dropped attention does not include anyone else; it is "just you and you."

If we practice these attentional states we will find that one is more difficult and one is easier for us to maintain. In my case, open attention is more difficult. So, I spend more time practicing with open attention. It is important for me to keep practicing so I can learn to be comfortable with this expansive state.

Chapter Eleven

Splits

Each of us is something of a schizophrenic personality, tragically divided against ourselves.

Martin Luther King, Jr.

A split is a separation or division within ourselves. In most cases it is a separation from the part of the body that relates to sensation and feeling. Our mental process can also be split; we can have the experience of being "of two minds." Distraction, fragmentation, and confusion are all forms of splits. Any situation in which we are not unified falls in this category.

Most of us who are working on ourselves have complex lives and our attention is often split because there are so many demands put upon us. We try to cover all our bases by putting our attention in two or more places at once. The result, of course, is a weakened, split state. The worst-case scenario is when we fight ourselves: our head wants to do one thing and our heart wants to do another. And so we work like crazy to get something done, but we become bogged down because one part of our energy will be going in one direction while another part goes in a different direction. We are putting out a lot of effort and not getting anywhere while life seems frustrating and exhausting.

I will give you an example of how this kind of split can occur. My mother-in-law is planning to visit soon, and I know that I should call to find out the exact dates of her visit so that I can plan time to see her while she is here. Yet I do not make the call because my heart and *hara*, my feeling and knowing centers, do not want to make contact with this person. My mind, on the other hand, knows that the proper thing to do is to make the arrangements. My mind also knows that if I do not do so, the situation will worsen and more negativity will be created. Because of the resistance or the split between my different centers, I am both unable to make the call and unable to make the decision not to call.

When I have an immobilizing experience like this, the first thing I try to do is to find out where I am split. When I feel that I am putting forward a lot of effort and yet nothing is happening, I assume that there are parts of me going in opposing directions. My task is to try to find out which parts are out of alignment. Once I can get in touch with the conflicted aspects of myself, I try to dialogue with them to bring them into alignment with each other.

As we get older, we develop another reason for splitting off— the habit of being weak. If we do not split off, we become unified, and with this unity we are more powerful. Most of us are really frightened by the idea of being more powerful. Even though we think we want power our systems are not accustomed to it. Power makes us more visible and, ironically, more vulnerable to the opinions and judgments of other people. So we sabotage ourselves—we do not reconcile our split state because it feels safer and more familiar. We may have moments where we become unified, but are not able to maintain them because our system is not accustomed to that type of clarity. Many people say that they have touched the enlightened state, but cannot stay there: it is just too powerful. When we want to discover where our splits are, the first thing to do is to recognize the feelings and signs of being split. One reliable sign of being split is when we are not getting the result that we would expect for the amount of energy we are expending. Basically this means that some part of us is pulling away.

On the aikido mat, I have found that when my partners are split, even a little bit, I can enter into that crack and stop or resist them— even someone weighing 100 pounds more than me. On the other hand, when my partners are unified, it becomes impossible to resist them even if they are very small. The interesting part about it is that when my partners are unified, I do not have much desire or interest in resisting them. When they are split, on the other hand, it draws out the devil in me. It is as if that crack, that weakness, sucks me in.

Basic Splits in the Body

In searching for the splits we can use a map with three centers: head, heart, and *hara,* or belly. Splits commonly occur at two places: either at the neck, separating the head from the heart and the belly, or the solar plexus, separating the belly from the heart and the head.

To find out where the split is, I focus individually on each of the three basic centers. I can usually identify the preferences of my head center with the question, "What do I think I want?" I wait for a sensory response. Then I feel into my heart, "What does my heart really feel like it wants?" and wait again. "Does my heart want the same thing as my head or not?" Sometimes the answer is "yes" and sometimes "no." My responses to these questions will give me some clues right away. If we are not aware of the opposition within ourselves, we may find it difficult to understand why we cannot bring something into a manifest action even when we have a clear idea about it.

Splits at the solar plexus are more difficult to discover. In Western culture, we are not accustomed to viewing the belly as an intelligent power source. Again, we might find it difficult to understand why, if we think and feel so strongly about something, we are not able to take action or feel completely satisfied about a situation. In relationship, we sometimes want to be closer to the other person, we crave more intimacy and more love. Yet, at the same time, we feel claustrophobic and want more distance. This ambivalence indicates a split at the solar plexus: our heart says "yes," while our belly says "no."

Disembodiment

Disembodiment is a shift of awareness away from the body. When we remove ourselves from the bodily sensations, we distance ourselves from the situation to which those sensations are related. An interesting aspect of disembodiment is that we may see, think, and function with a clear and precise intellectual capacity, while lacking any bodily sensations to accompany our mental activities. This state is sometimes described as feeling numb. Disembodiment is a strategy that allows us to escape the pressure, feeling, or sensations of the present moment. With this style of behavior, we can function correctly but there is no feeling, no quality of satisfaction.

Disembodiment is common in people who have had histories of psychological and physical abuse, such as incest. For many survivors of abuse, their survival mechanism was to abandon their body and seek refuge as an outside observer who watches but does not feel. Many of us have had this experience in lovemaking. If we shift away from the sensation and move into the observer, we derive less satisfaction from the experience.

In early childhood, a child's desire for sensate contact and the accompanying energetic intensity can often be overwhelming to the parent. When the child makes these energetic demands, the parent may become angry and negative or withdraw altogether from the child. Subsequently, when the child withdraws his or her energy and begins to relate mentally, the parent gives love and support. This trains the child toward disembodiment, and this split bears a heavy legacy. If we cannot tolerate sensations and feelings, we can become cold and calculating. Usually when feelings and sensations become too intense, either too painful or too pleasurable, we split off from ourselves. Splitting makes us less effective, but it also serves to make us feel less uncomfortable.

The Observer

When teaching basic practice, I always say, "lose the observer into sensation." This encourages us to have the experience of what it is like to be unified inside our bodies without a part of ourselves split off, looking in or down at ourselves in action. When we receive satisfaction in making love or are fully engaged in a creative activity, we are usually immersed in the sensations without part of ourselves commenting on the process.

I am not suggesting that being immersed in the sensation without an observer is the right or only way to proceed, but I do suggest that we want to be able to experience things in this way. We need to be flexible. When we rest the mind in the center of the present, we can explore the possibility of functioning skillfully and compassionately without the mind always reporting, commenting, and judging our actions. We need to find out whether this state is trustworthy and satisfying, and if it is, we want to be able to evoke this state at will.

Chögyam Trungpa's perception of this phenomenon may be helpful in understanding the observer:

> There is a watcher which transmits its message to the observer as opposed to the watcher. So you have a double watcher in that case. You have a watcher who is like the spokesman who relates from one situation to another situation; you also have the person who appointed the watcher to his occupation, his job, his duty. In other words you have intuitive insight, which has the ability to digest experiences, but at the same time, you have to point them out to somebody who collects the food. That which is collecting food is the watcher and the food is being passed on to the central authority who appointed the watcher. This is extremely subtle. It is almost non-watching— a perceiving entity, so to speak. So you have two types of intelligence there. Crude intelligence and subtle intelligence. Crude intelligence is the watcher, the analyst; subtle intelligence is the intellectual, analytical conclusions transformed into experiential understanding.
>
> —from *Transcending Madness*

We want to know what it is like to have no observer and experience the mind as still, not spaced out—a feeling of being awake, precise, and clearly present. The sensation is the reference point. We are that sensation without any judgment or commentary. Losing the observer is something we want to be able to do, ***even for one second.*** Even a brief moment without the observer is an important and valuable experience. And we can practice and repeat this experience again and again. As we become more familiar with the experience of becoming the sensation, we can come to it more quickly, and stay in it longer.

The next step is to find out if we can be active without the observer. To find out, we have to enter the state itself. When I say, "lose the observer in sensation," I am calling for us to suspend the commentator/judge and asking to be right here in the center of the present in a wakeful and unified way.

Three Centers: Head, Heart, and *Hara*

To mobilize my thoughts, I have to spark interest: I ask the right question so that I am magnetized into the head center. Mentally, I have to be more interested than afraid. Remember the whole idea of curiosity. I need to be sure that I am not entering into the head center in order to take control of the situation. I must enter with a genuine interest in simply seeing what it is like there. This is where we use our discipline and training. We focus our thoughts, think about one thing and ask, "What is at the center of this situation?"

To move from the heart center, we must yearn for contact. There is a sense of surrender, of being drawn in, like being in love. The heart must be courageous. If we have done our groundwork and realize that we cannot protect ourselves by keeping things out, then we can move in, without trying to avoid contact. We move in as if we are in love: we take the whole package, the whole person, not just his or her positive sides, but the negative aspects as well. When we accept our own fear, our heart allows contact and we are drawn in—we experience intimacy.

To be connected with and move from the *hara*, or belly, we have to make a physical embodied commitment within space. We bring the ideas from the head and the feelings from the heart into manifest action. Moving from the *hara* means actually getting up off our duffs and moving our bodies; we make a physical change within space. In the actual "doing" of an act, we can discover the truth of its worth. We can find out where we are split and where our fear resides. Doing the actual physical practice is the way to find out the truth of our situation. The *hara* moves the body, and when we allow it, the belly will demonstrate its vitality and wisdom.

Techniques Toward Unification: Healing the Split

The first step toward unification is to gather our attention. Basic practice: breath, balance, and gravity, can restore our awareness of body presence. As we evoke our quality, the head center is connected to our body through the spirit of inquiry. We engage our interest in our sensate experience of the present moment by asking the question: "What would it be like if _____?"

One of my favorite techniques to reconnect my heart and *hara* is "stroking." Using the palms of my hands, I stroke from my heart down to my belly the same way I might stroke an animal in an affectionate, soft manner. This "stroking" gives a direct sensate connection between the heart and the belly. It is also soothing and relaxing.

We can also dialogue with our centers. I spend a few moments focusing on a particular center. For instance, to focus on my head, I might touch my forehead and really analyze the situation. Immediately, I write down the essential point of view from my head center, writing in a stream-of-consciousness style. I am not analyzing or judging the writing—I just allow it to flow out. Next, I put my hand on my heart, bringing my awareness there so I can get the feel of the situation. When I feel that I have made contact with my heart center, I again write down the "message" in a stream-of-consciousness style. Then I do the same with my belly center. Often the "voice" or message from the belly is harder to hear, but if I put my hand on my belly, breathe into it and relax, it is possible to make contact with this part of myself. When practicing this technique, just let the writing flow out, it does not have to make perfect sense. When we read it over we will get the gist of it.

When I am feeling split, I may repeat this exercise several times over a period of a few days. Often, the more I do it, the more clear the messages become. Once the nature of the inner conflict has become clear, I can begin the process of dialogue. The goal is to bring all three centers into agreement. It may sound strange, but I have gone so far as to bargain with my centers. For instance, I may ask my belly to support my heart for the sake of unification. I assure my *hara* that next time I will let it have precedence and ask my heart to go along with it. For the most part it seems better to be unified than to be "right."

Override

Override is probably the most common method we use to deal with splits. It occurs as an act of will: the mind overrides the heart or the mind drags the heart and belly along. Override will work, but it is tiring and stressful for one part to have to drag another part along all of the time. When we operate in override, the amount of energy required to maintain it is exhausting and life seems like a struggle. If we can convince the other centers to come along willingly, they become supportive and it takes less energy and less force to get things accomplished.

Often our splits and conflicts are obvious, sometimes they are not. By studying ourselves under pressure and/or in movement with a partner, we can usually quickly figure out how we split or separate from ourselves. By having compassion, humor, and doing basic practice, we can train ourselves toward unification.

How Do I Know When I Am Unified?

Many of us are doubters or perfectionists and may feel that we are never truly centered or unified. Here are some signs to let us know we are in the right area.

When we are unified, we have:

- awareness of breath
- sensations of gravity
- softness and alertness in our bodies
- an internal feeling of clarity and focus

Part IV

Embodied
Action

Chapter Twelve

Irimi

Strength has more to do with intention than with the size of your biceps. It has more to do with your Spirit and your energy flow than the number of push-ups you can do.

Terry Dobson

The concept of *irimi* is translated as "entering." *Irimi* is an embracing of life, a fundamental urge of our being. We perceive *irimi* in conception: the sperm swims toward the egg, a moving into life with the desire to connect, move toward, and penetrate while the receptive egg waits with its ability to accept, include, and hold that which comes. These two forces balance the universal life force and are described in different cosmologies as *yin* and *yang*, positive and receptive, masculine and feminine, father and mother. The *irimi* of inquiry is the mind's movement into the nature of being. *Irimi* is the sense of commitment and precision used to focus and direct the energy to the heart of the matter.

The Spirit of *Irimi*

In aikido, *irimi* is the act of entering directly into an attack. In sixteenth-century Japan, the *yagyu* school of swordsmanship used a technique called *marubashi,* which is translated as "the bridge of life."

As the enemy attacks cutting with his sword, movement is neither to the left nor to the right, but directly into the path of the attack, cutting in one timing through his sword and through his spirit. It is a technique of entering and choosing death.

The philosophy which underlies this technique perceives life as a narrow log spanning a torrential river. As one comes face to face with the enemy in the middle of the bridge, there is no escape. To retreat or even hesitate is to be cut down by the sword ... choosing life is death.

The only path is the enemy's path. There must be no separation but an exchange of time and space with the spirit of moving into the very heart of the enemy. This is the spirit of *Irimi*.... Only by abandoning attachment to time and space, attachment to life, will true freedom of choosing death be attained ... choosing death is life.

—Mitsugi Saotome, *Aikido and the Harmony of Nature*

So what does it mean to choose death? By choosing death, how can we choose life? There is a story about a young man who seeks out a swordmaster to teach him the skills of swordsmanship:

A young man went to a swordmaster and asked to be accepted as a student.

"I am sorry to offer you this poor student who has no skill with the sword, but please accept me for the people in my village have no one but me to defend them."

The swordmaster invited the young man to stand opposite him with his sword.

After a short time the swordmaster lowered his sword and said: "You have been dishonest with me. You are a master."

"No," replied the young man. "I know nothing."

"Your feeling is that of a master," said the swordmaster. "Tell me, what have you done?"

"Since my skill with the sword was so poor, I thought that I would be killed very quickly, so every day I practiced facing and accepting my death."

"Ah!" said the swordmaster. "Truly you are a master—a master of your self, and I can teach you very quickly. Technique is easy. Accepting death is the most difficult part and you have already accomplished that."

Irimi is the act of entering into life—not trying to avoid it. *Irimi* is a way of consciously exploring our fear that provides an opportunity to understand what holds us back and prevents us from living fully. What are some of the elements that help us to face our fear, to open our hearts, and move forward into life?

It seems to me that the two most important elements for facing our fear are ground and interest. We begin with groundedness because it provides a place from which we can then become interested. When there is a sense of embodied stability, it allows a settling down that provides some space in our being. Within that space interest and inquiry can arise. The inquiry is *irimi*. I often say, "If you are afraid of something, become interested in it." By entering into a situation, we may begin to change our experience of it. Fear often begins to dissipate at this point. There is an element of generosity here as well— we give ourselves to the moment, no holding back, no watching or observing from the outside. We make a complete surrender into the moment.

When I introduce the concept of *irimi* in a class, we do an exercise involving partners. The pairs begin by standing opposite each other. One person takes the role of the attacker and the other one is the person to be attacked. The attacker strikes and extends his or her fist into the belly of the partner. The attacker's clenched fist can represent anything: anger, aggression, criticism, intimacy, or other intense energetic states. The person being attacked moves to meet the fist, then pivots behind the attacker and duplicates the attacker's stance. The person who was being attacked ends up standing directly behind the attacker in a matching pose, seeing and feeling the situation from the attacker's perspective.

Repeating this exercise many times, we can study how we respond during moments of incoming aggression or intimacy. We begin to discover what it feels like to be in an embodied state or a way of being that allows us to be calm and move directly into the attack. We may also notice that most of the time our bodies try to avoid the attack. The repetition of this exercise lets us experience what happens in both situations. If we have enough groundedness and focus, we can penetrate through our defensiveness and not be distracted by fear, confusion, or other emotions.

Once the partner who receives the attack has moved in and is standing behind the attacker, the next step is to recognize how to match that energy. The matching is referred to as blending. We do not want to merge or get lost in the other person's energy. We want to be able to become like the other person, see the world from his or her point of view, while we retain our sense of self and our own sense of center.

A very important phenomenon occurs here. When we become similar to another person, they find it difficult to attack us. During class I explain, "Aggression depends upon duality: there must be a you and a me. If when I attack you, then you become similar to me, you are hard to locate and therefore hard to attack. This is what is meant by blending. You become like the person attacking you and he or she has no place to focus aggression." This phenomenon of blending with the attacker only occurs for a second or two, but it is a very important moment. As soon as the connection—the blend— is made, we make another shift, return to our center, and focus our attention on our own vision. If our vision is strong enough, the attacker is magnetized or drawn into our vision with us or the aggression is dissipated, and each person goes along his or her way.

A student told me a story which exemplifies the blending phenomenon quite well:

> On a beautiful Sunday morning I drove to a cafe to enjoy a cappuccino and was looking forward to reading a book. As I parked my car I noticed a man glaring at me. He wore no shirt except for a leather vest and had a webbed army belt from which hung a Bowie knife on one side and an ax on the other. As I observed his hostile stare, my first reaction was fear and stress. I also felt guilty that I might appear to him to be "yuppie scum." But I resented the guilt, the stress, and losing my sense of peace and appreciation for the day.
>
> Recalling the principles of aikido, I mentally pushed aside the thought that he and I were enemies. I refocused my assertion that I was neither his enemy nor his victim. With this

focus, stress left my body and I walked forward in his direction looking him in the eye.

He unsnapped the holster, took out his ax and held it in a menacing way. As I continued in his direction, he raised the ax as if aiming at my forehead. When I was within ten feet of the man I looked up at the ax and said, "Wow, that's really nice—double-headed and chrome-plated. You must be proud." At this point his hostile stare changed to one of aggravation. He slowly returned the ax to its holster and walked around me. I continued on in the direction of the cafe.

—Neil

Neil's story reflects the transformative power of openness and interest. It reminds us that we have other options besides "fight or flight." It takes courage and presence to remember these options, but if we are committed to growing into life we can develop these parts of ourselves.

Facing Our Fear

The practice of *irimi* can be used to handle internal aggression as well as outside aggression. When dealing with myself, I remember O Sensei said, "The attacker is not out there, but within," and use *irimi* to deal with myself.

When I am aggressive or negative toward myself, I can use the same technique I use in dealing with someone outside myself: I center and then I move in and blend. When I can accept myself and my own negativity, I can encourage myself toward a more positive view. If I am frightened or intimidated by my own self-hatred or afraid of my own loneliness and despair, I will try to escape or distract myself. In reality there is no escape and we end up having to come back and face ourselves—we face the sword.

I once asked a very special aikido teacher, Terry Dobson, if he was ever afraid when he was on the mat. His response was, "Yes, but I am accustomed to my fear." If we accept our fear and ground or stabilize, we can use the energy of the fear or pain. There is tremendous energy in fear and suffering. By doing basic practice, we can develop enough depth to accept and include these aspects of ourselves. Then, we can begin to accept these elements in other people. Acceptance is the basis of compassion. Compassion allows us to open our hearts so that we can be drawn into the very center of the situation. We can use *irimi* as a way of not giving up or copping out. Inspiration is our greatest protection. The act of moving in, of entering into life, is an inspired action.

Another student witnessed the power of this phenomenon in class one day:

> From the time I was five until I was fourteen, I was sexually molested by my father. Why should I support my attacker? I thought: No way. I am here to take care of me and no one is going to touch me. After fourteen years of therapy, I still could not access the area around my pelvis as something other than a place of pain and rage.
>
> One day in class, Wendy and I were face-to-face about to do the *irimi* exercise. She moved to attack me and I pivoted around behind her like I had been taught.
>
> She said, "You are doing the moves right, but you are not supporting me. You need to support your attacker. Are you willing to truly support me?"
>
> I said, "No."
>
> She waited. Then she said, "Are you willing to be hurt, for me to hit you?"
>
> I stood there and said, "No, no way."
>
> One of the people observing us was my bereavement counselor and he said: "She has had enough pain in her life."
>
> Wendy stood there and would not move. I realized that the game was up. If I did not support her and give up my need to protect myself from being hurt, I would not get anywhere.
>
> Wendy stood there.
>
> She said, "It's better to love and to be hurt than to not love. It is better to be willing to love again and to be hurt again."
>
> I realized that this was a turning point in my life. Later I asked her to hit me in the stomach and I realized that it did not hurt so much. It was just my fear. And I survived.
>
> —Susan

Evolving by Manageable Percentages

Initially, we enter into a situation to experience it with a willingness to penetrate through to what is essential. I have observed that for people to evolve they have to be a little hungry. This hunger is what makes a team win in sports. Hunger means that we are willing to go through some discomfort for our goal. If we are on overload, we do not want any more suffering, we do not want any more information, we do not want any more anything. Overload is a survival mechanism. Someone on overload is full and they are not hungry.

True *irimi* is not trying to escape injury. Instead, we are willing to be injured and move in anyway. At the beginning of each series of classes, I usually ask, "Is it possible to protect yourself?" What I am asking about is the sense of making ourselves safe from harm. In my experience, protecting ourselves is not really possible, and, in my belief, protecting ourselves is not the point. The point is to keep living in a way that is compassionate, skillful, and creative. Being hurt is not a terrible thing—it is a fact of life. We can experience hurt and still go forward with an open heart. We can go ahead even though we are afraid to move. We do not have to wait until we are healed to love.

To be able to go forward at a manageable rate, we need to move in increments that will not put our system on overload. In Western culture, high achievement is respected—the younger we are and the faster things are accomplished, the better. We need to reeducate ourselves to consider one- to three-percent increases as positive and effective change, rather than as failure. Our internal systems organize themselves around homeostatic response; that is, we become easily habituated. Any extreme change sends our systems into overload and we have an impulse to return to what is habitual. We need to develop ourselves in increments that will not send our systems into a state of overwhelm.

Instead of thinking about all that we have not yet achieved, what would it be like to say, "I am one percent or three percent better. This is great." When the government raises taxes a quarter of a percent it is thought of as a major increase. If we were to get a five-percent pay raise we would be pleased. It is important to remember that small increments are movement toward success—anything that is more is helpful. And yet, if we advance three percent in our positive relationship to ourselves, the typical response is to focus on what we have not yet accomplished. These one- to three-percent increases do have a cumulative effect overall. We can take little bites because they are movement in the right direction. We need to develop a positive coach for ourselves.

Counterphobia

> Challenge is the correct way to view an inconvenience; an
> inconvenience is the incorrect way to view a challenge.
> —Zen Buddhist aphorism

A phobia is a "fear of" something. When people have phobic feelings about something, they stay away from whatever it is that scares them. On the other hand, those who are counterphobic rush toward the things they fear. To the external world counterphobic people look courageous and powerful. While counterphobics feel no fear, there is no courage, no sense of awareness either, only a knee-jerk reaction to bolt forward with a vague sense of attacking or controlling that which is before them.

Counterphobic individuals have a sense of blankness and tension, often followed by surprise at actually having arrived somewhere. Because counterphobics cannot feel that they are afraid, they have to look for signs of fear by studying their actions. Once counterphobics realize that their entering movement is a compulsive reaction rather than a centered, soft movement to the heart of things, they can begin the task of slowing down; they can soften and notice the rush of energy that precedes their movement. The idea is to tolerate the rushes of energy, often experienced as fear, and move forward with an open heart and clear perception. Courage is being conscious of our fear and still going forward.

In class, we often practice *irimi* with a wooden sword. I stand poised with the sword and muster my best aggressive energy as the students come before me one by one. As I strike at them, they enter. I can always tell the counterphobic types because they tend to actually bump into me when they are entering, in a primitive version of "attack the attacker." Even though they are entering in, the tension that they carry with them stimulates my aggression, and I usually want to shove them out of my way. A phobic person, on the other hand, tries to dodge or escape the blow. The wide berth that the phobic person uses to avoid the sword is like a magnet that draws my aggression, like a fly to flypaper. When the person who is being attacked keeps his or her energy relaxed, centered, and direct, my aggressive focus is softened and my concentration wavers.

The *Irimi* of Questioning

An article I read about the fear of nuclear war told of a man who was terrified of nuclear war as a child. Eventually this man became a nuclear physicist. His father had advised him, "When you are afraid of something, learn everything you can about it." This is *irimi*. The more afraid I am, the more I try to understand what it is I am afraid of. Asking a question is *irimi*—it penetrates and takes us in. If I learn to ask myself the right question, then I can draw myself into something that I might otherwise be pulling away from or contracting against. The fine art of questioning, of asking the right question, is an essential part of the process.

It is important to know that we can use the spirit of inquiry in a counterproductive way. We can move ourselves further away from something by asking the wrong questions and set ourselves up to fail. Inappropriate questions keep us from discovering our forward-moving and positive aspects, and further distract us from ourselves.

An essential part of the internal process is how to develop our line of questioning. It is important to stay fresh and up-to-date with ourselves. The questions I asked myself four years ago may not have the same amount of interest or impact anymore. The old questions may be in reference to the same old issues, but I have to rephrase them to keep myself current with my internal process. This is all *irimi*—moving forward and toward something at the same time.

There is a sense of fullness and fascination that I associate with *irimi*. The positiveness and forward movement connotes an ecstatic willingness to experience life. *Irimi* contains both stillness and activity with a vigilance to adhere to the precision of the moment, entering into the heart and soul of the situation, penetrating into the marrow of the moment. Past and future are suspended, held, and we are included in the experience of now. The feeling of *irimi* is organic, the way a plant moves toward the sun; entering, the way the young shoots will reach and stretch up out of the darkness into the light. Our base, our grounded center, is like a well-established root system that moves upward even in its stillness when it is fed by the rich compost of our suffering and watered by the compassion of our caring hearts.

The intention of "about to" combined with not-knowing produces a magnetic pull toward positive movement. There is the precision of a clear movement forward in which the entire system— body, mind, and emotions—is involved from the basis of attraction. This attraction compels any resistant or renegade parts to be drawn into the movement. As our vision becomes more precise, we can penetrate through resistance more easily.

Without a vision of our purpose, we have the tendency to merge or be drawn off by the elements we are encountering and our movement is weakened or neutralized. Our vision is the intention of our spirit. Our intention can be about accomplishing something or just being precisely in the moment of "nowness." When we lose our *irimi* quality, we lose our sense of being present in the moment. There can be no precision because we are fragmented and scattered over the future and the past, acting without consciousness. Just the act of collecting ourselves, of becoming present, is an act of *irimi* or entering—entering into wakefulness.

Irimi is connection: movement into genuine contact with some aspect of the circumstance, without any agenda or wanting to change the person or situation. When we contact what is at the deepest possible level, we are able to move to the next level of what is affecting us.

In aikido, when a person moves to grab my wrist, I shift my weight and intention slightly forward. I do not wait for my partner to contact me; I contact my partner. We both have the intention to make contact at the deepest, most essential level possible. If, as I shift forward toward my partner, I have a sensate connection to my belly, legs, and feet, then the quality of my contact will include those parts of me. If my desire to contact my partners includes their hand, heart, belly, legs and feet, then we will be intensely connected for the amount of time that we can jointly hold the concentration. Usually our attention will shift or flicker toward the future, but while we maintain the connection, it is an intense and intimate moment.

As our capacity for kinesthetic concentration grows, our capacity for deep intimate contact also grows. Combined with the intention to penetrate, to move into the action, or more generally into life, our capacity for contact helps develops *irimi* ability. Speed and timing begin to develop intuitively as we continue to train, practice, and bring ourselves forward to meet life's situations again and again. Timing comes from relaxation. Relaxation comes from confidence. Confidence comes from experience.

As our curiosity, interest, and fascination are cultivated, our presence and precision grow as well. When our mind, heart, and belly are all brought into the moment of connection, we have entered into the state of penetration. We are entering the mystery. The unfolding has begun.

Chapter Thirteen

Different Approaches

With your spirit settled, accumulate practice day by day, and hour by hour. Polish the two-fold spirit, heart and mind, and sharpen the two-fold gaze, perception and sight. When your spirit is not the least bit clouded, when the clouds of bewilderment clear away, there is the true void.

Miyamoto Musashi

The Masculine—The Motivating Force

What can we use as a motivating force? How can we train ourselves to move forward into the present? How do we deal with situations when the road is blocked and it seems that we cannot move forward? What of those moments when we seem to be backsliding, away from our goal?

In dealing with this aspect of the path, it is helpful to know that everyone is confronted with the experiences that are the basis of these questions. They are, in fact, part of the process of spiritual growth. It helps if our mind, our rational part, has the concept of spiritual growth in place. Our feeling body may still experience betrayal, bewilderment, or pain, but our mind understands that these experiences are inevitable and necessary parts of the process. In his book *Mastery*, George Leonard has mapped out some of the obstacles that we may meet along the path. The knowledge is helpful in giving us hope and assists us in finding a way to continue.

At another time or in a slightly altered situation, our knowledge and mental understanding may be of no use at all; every thought may be blocked with a counter-thought, an existential thought. At these times it may be the heart's turn to provide the motivation or the strength to continue. It may make absolutely no sense whatsoever, but we have a feeling, a longing, a desire to connect to life. Our more devotional side emerges. We may feel like a blind person feeling our way forward.

Another possibility is that our belly, our *hara,* or action center, becomes responsible for our forward movement. The accompanying sensation is that of "just doing it" without having to understand it. We may not even feel we are on the right track. We just do it. We may find ourselves either sitting down to meditate or getting up to do our movement practice.

When we make a commitment to our spiritual path, it usually stems from our longing to abate our suffering and genuine altruistic feelings for other beings. As we do our practice each day, we are renewing this commitment. Our intention to focus ourselves and become unified represents the effort to work directly with our tendency toward suffering which is created by our inner conflict.

When we are doing one thing at a time, concentrating on just our breath, gravity, our field, and our quality—for those few seconds we are not in conflict. During those moments, in a certain sense, we are abating suffering and promoting harmony in the world. We want to use as much of ourselves as possible toward this end. One way to do this is to unify ourselves by contacting each center, head, heart and hara, and enlisting their support.

By encouraging our sense of interest we can encourage our head center, our mind, to keep asking questions that draw us into our practice. Training the mind to the habit of inquiry helps us to develop openmindedness. We need to be gentle in our inquiry so that we do not encourage the habit of grasping and holding on to knowledge. We need to move toward a state of mental calmness and clarity so that our interest can have a penetrating, precise quality. In order to calm our minds, we learn to control our tendency to race around from one habitual thought pattern to another training our minds to focus on just one thing at a time.

We train our minds by practicing and by returning our attention over and over again to the object of concentration. In class I say, "You will know it when you are able to do it. You will feel the mind steady itself. You will feel its readiness, its capacity to be open and curious." This calmness is usually achieved through meditation practice that has a particular time set aside for just this purpose. The act of remembering to practice during the day helps bring this experience to our natural way of being. We know that we have a technique, a tool that will help us to focus our mind.

It is important to be able to separate our thoughts from our feelings because this separation allows us to identify any inherent conflict between the head and the heart. Sometimes it is easy to see the conflict in a situation where fear is the resistant ingredient. As an example, I am scheduled to speak in front of a group of people. Perhaps the material is very familiar and I really want to communicate the information to the audience. My feeling part, my heart, is experiencing fear and resistance. I may even feel that I absolutely cannot get up in front of all those people. In this instance, I have conflict between my head and heart centers which makes it extremely difficult to mobilize myself to action. Recognizing the conflict is the first step. The next step is to use a technique, a tool, that helps me bring my heart into alignment with my head. It is also possible to bring my head into alignment with my heart. What is really important is unification—finding a way to terminate the conflict by bringing the centers into agreement.

The heart center's great capacity for devotion uses feeling, longing, desire, passion, and need as its motivating energies. In order to use this powerful internal force, we must find a way to harness or direct these energies. With persistent inquiry, we can locate our essential altruistic urge, our deep desire for union with life, our wish to feel connected. We can direct our inquiries toward a goal that is consistent with our mental vision, or draw our mind into alignment with our heart, our desire for love, kindness, and beauty. We have to be able to distinguish between distorted needs and desires and genuine essential urges.

We can steady our heart center by slowing down, paying attention, and taking the time to do the practices that focus on one feeling at a time. With practice, we can burn like a steady flame exuding
passion, compassion, kindness, or other heart energies. We are no
longer like a flickering flame being blown about by the winds of distorted desire and confusion. When there is a calmness, a steadiness
in our feelings, we can begin to open ourselves to our strong feelings. We are cultivating open-heartedness and can use the energy of
the heart center to bring us more deeply into life.

The *hara*, or belly center, is frequently the most difficult center
to locate in terms of its motivating force. The one exception to this
is sexual desire which is actually located below the *hara*, but can be
included as part of this center because it has a clear impulse toward
action and a desire for consummation. Our *hara* provides the energy
for the "doing" part of our life. The belly is the part of us that does.
Our *hara* gets us up out of the chair; we enlist its power to push a
car. The belly desires union in the most active, embodied sense. Our
head may think that it is a good idea to walk over and say hello to
someone. Our heart may feel a desire to do so. But it is our belly
that moves us across the room and places us in embodied contact
with another person. The belly is about the manifestation of desire
or thought.

When we recognize this and move from the belly, a sense of confidence begins to develop within us. Western culture has created certain taboos around personal power and sexual energy. These taboos
have resulted in an obscuring of our connection to our bellies. The
pain of incest and other forms of abuse has taught many of us to hide
and bury our sense of confidence and power. To uncover and reclaim
this part of ourselves takes patience, courage, and interest. Only
when we can make an intimate connection to our *hara* can we discover whether it is in conflict or harmony with our heart and head.
We can unify ourselves only if we have access to the parts that we
are bringing together.

By understanding something about how these parts function or
do not function, we can create strategies to assist ourselves through

the hard times. There are inevitable periods when our path takes us through the foothills and we lose sight of the mountain peak we want to reach. We need to recognize that we are in the foothills. We must remember that sometimes the closer we get to where we want to go, the harder it is to see where that is. Since we cannot see it or understand it any more, we must be able to feel it. In the moment when we cannot even feel it, we need to be able to draw on our capacity to keep on going and do it anyway. We can mobilize and keep going until our inspiration returns.

Having a goal, moving toward it, and learning how it mobilizes us in embodied action represents one half of our essential nature. It is the *yang*, the "masculine," the doing part of ourselves. Now, let's take a look at the other side and explore some of the possibilities of non-action.

The Feminine and Non-Action

The capacity to *be*, without doing, is a particularly exquisite experience in life—we accept life exactly how it is. We are still, present, alert, open, and receptive to any minute changes that occur within our field of awareness. I associate the "feminine" quality with a circular shape and an element of spaciousness in which there is room for all kinds of things to occur. The feminine has been referred to as the Great Mother or the Mystery. There is a sense of the feminine as being the source—the place from which action arises. Action comes out of non-action, springing forth from the stillness of being, the emptiness of no-thought. This ability to hold the space, to be, to not do, is the power of the feminine. My favorite verse of the *Tao Te Ching* speaks of it this way:

> *The valley spirit is not dead.*
> *They say it is the mystic female.*
> *Her gateway is, they further say,*
> *The base of heaven and earth.*
> *Constantly and so forever,*
> *Use her without labor.*
> —Lao Tzu, *Tao Te Ching* #6

This inexhaustible source, which is in all of us, is almost completely misunderstood or overlooked in our achievement-oriented culture. When we quiet ourselves into stillness, we may be accused of being lazy. Laziness, in my opinion, is not inaction but rather inattention. Acceptance is the ability to be with exactly what is—to hold the space for it, without trying to change it or transform it. Tremendous depth is required to keep including each moment as it arises. We often have a very strong tendency to want to interfere, to make it better, to fix it, transform it. The feminine has the capacity to let things be as they are and to continually expand the boundaries of being. To do this, we need a great sense of curiosity—we have to be truly interested in what will arise, open to any possibility without trying to mold it, or make it be a certain way. Instead of penetrating the mystery, we allow ourselves to be penetrated by the mystery.

How can we surrender in a way that feels life-giving? At what point do we perceive penetration as violation? To explore these questions, we must first be aware of and establish distinct boundaries. When our boundaries are clarified, we can focus on the moment and the experience of penetration. The feminine allows itself to be penetrated. Ideally, we have developed enough base or depth to be able to accept, even welcome, the energy into our being. We do not have to stiffen against the energy, collapse or run away from it. In this ideal state, we are like a mother accepting the child into our arms. The power of receiving and accepting is most fully known when when we are interacting with its counterpart—the action-oriented masculine, that which penetrates.

Balance: Integrating the Masculine and the Feminine

To study the interaction of masculine and feminine energies, we can use an aikido style of practicing with positive and receptive energies. In aikido, the *uke* is the partner who attacks and is thrown and the *nage* is the partner who receives the attack and throws. *Uke* begins the action and mobilizes in a specific way. The goal is to penetrate to and control *nage's* center. *Nage* must receive, accept, or include the *uke's* energy or intention. Up until this point, *uke* is masculine, penetrating, and *nage* is receptive, feminine. Then there is a rather mystical, magical moment in which the situation reverses itself. (I will discuss this spiral moment in more detail in the next section.) *Nage* now penetrates *uke*, who receives the energy and is usually thrown through the air, at which point the energy is again converted into a positive action. This positive action allows *uke* to fall or land skillfully without injury. Phwew! All of this can take place in one to three seconds.

The dance between masculine and feminine is a natural, organic process that is happening even as these words are being read. In order to educate ourselves to understand and appreciate this dance, we must look very carefully at the increments of the continuum. Following the aikido metaphor, we ask, "When I attack as *uke*, can I surrender my body to the *nage*? Can I give myself as fully as possible to meet the situation?" The real challenge is to suspend any ideas or perceived notions, to risk being hurt, in order to gain an extraordinary awareness in which everything becomes pertinent and connected. In the moment of being, we are fully absorbed and gathered into the power of the throw. Can we initiate the task? Can we move from the masculine and then suspend our ideas, surrender to the not-knowing in the feminine realm, to see what kind of insight, experience, or child will come forth?

It takes training, courage, and concentration to stay right in the middle of the present unfolding moment. Instead, what frequently occurs is that we try to take back control of the situation and shift our attention into the future. The masculine intention, the desire to know, often overlays the feminine, the not-knowing, the mystery. The result is that the feminine aspect is cut short, or cut off altogether. A whole part of ourselves is lost, buried under our knowledge. And so we lead half-lives, yearning for wholeness and satisfaction, often not understanding what is missing.

I believe that we can reclaim ourselves and learn to move back and forth between the mastery of the masculine and the mystery of the feminine. Through practice and patient training, we can become more familiar with the subtleties and nuances of the dance. We can recognize the different ways of being while allowing ourselves to participate in them more fully. We want to develop the ability to be hard and sharp and then soft and open. When each possibility is available, both our intuition and our creative part, we can make a natural organic choice and shift in a millisecond. Then in this dance anything is possible.

The Magical Turnaround

Earlier I alluded to the moment when the energy of the attacker, *uke*, is reversed. At that moment the *uke* receives the energy of the *nage*, the one who throws. When this move is executed correctly, the attacker experiences a sensation akin to astonishment or awe. Neither the physical nor the intellectual parts of us can process or digest the experience of total acceptance fast enough to organize against it or separate from it. In order for conflict to exist, for the attack to consummate itself, there has to be a duality: a "you" and a "me." Someone has to attack someone else and someone has to defend himself or herself against the attack. At the moment when the *nage* fully accepts, agrees, and includes the *uke*, the duality, separation, and conflict cease to exist. This is the blend. Precisely in the middle of the blend is when the *nage's* energy is transformed from receptive to positive and in that same instant *uke's* energy shifts from positive to receptive.

Sounds easy enough, and the concept is not obscure, but the embodiment of it is something else altogether. To accept the other person's power or intention fully, we need tremendous depth and an incredibly strong center that can hold and tolerate the energy of another without needing to take control or losing our balance. We need to be calm, loving, open, and able to perceive an eighth of a second as plenty of time as we accept the attack, so we can feel the attacker's energy shift, become open, then confused, when he finds nothing to go against. At that instant, we intend with our whole being the direction in which we would like the *uke* to move. Our focus is so clear that it is like a magnet drawing the energy of *uke* towards our internal goal. The *uke* is amazed to find himself or herself flat on the mat.

Because this happened through acceptance and magnetism there is no hurt, only amazement. For those who have experienced this or something like it, it is an exquisite sensation. Ego and aggression are suspended and the natural movement between positive and receptive, masculine and feminine, flows like our breath. Inside the vortex of swirling movement, we can feel and enjoy the sensations of intense power and gentleness. We can relinquish control and be moved by the breath of life.

Discovering Aspects of Our Being

As we explore the potential of our creative and intuitive selves, we can evoke different aspects of ourselves to see how they would handle different situations. If we pay attention as we approach a task, we can notice that a certain aspect of ourselves comes forward, or leads our body into the movement. For instance, if I am going to bring some very heavy packages from my car into the house, a somewhat stronger aspect of myself moves toward the car, a stronger aspect than if I were going to sit and relax in the garden.

There is an interesting movement practice that involves walking and leading from different points of view. Of the many points of view, some particularly informative ones include our warrior, our adult (our man or woman), and our child. In doing this exercise, I uncovered some helpful things about myself. First, leading from my warrior was familiar and had a sharp, pointed quality. As I began evoking my woman or my adult, I found a softness and calmness about her. As I asked my child to come forward, I found a blank— my system did not know how to bring her out. I want to point out that I could access my wounded, angry child, but I could not find the open, playful child. She was obscured in a haze of uncertainty.

As we continued to explore these parts of ourselves in class, I began to learn more about my woman. Her shape tends to be round and there is a quiet evenness about her. I even began to sense that her hair was dark and her skin very fair. Instead of the light blue quality I often associate with myself, my woman has a soft rosy sense about her. She feels very capable and spacious. I have found that at times when I do not want to or cannot do something, my woman is ready and willing to come forward to meet the task at hand. I have to use concentration and discipline to ask her to come forward, and then I have to be willing to focus on her and empower her. My woman is a part of myself that usually does not come forward because my warrior is too busy dominating the scene.

My warrior tends to be a strong, no-nonsense character, intent on getting the job done. This part of me wants to have integrity and be impeccable. My warrior's underlying theme is, "don't give up." The shape of my warrior feels more like a wedge or a blade. There is a masculine quality to this aspect of myself and I tend to refer to it as "he." My warrior has a strong sense of autonomy and functions best when operating out of an intuitive mode, rather than a mental idea about what should be done.

Because I am interested in what each of these aspects is like, I elicit the details about their shape, size, look, and feel. The more I am open to them, the more they come to life. Then, I can explore the possibility of meeting the tasks of life with more options. I can use my curiosity, "How would my woman respond to this?" "How would my warrior?" "My child?" Sometimes it is obvious that one aspect of myself is better suited to deal with a situation than another. When they are all available, it is fascinating to see which one will arise spontaneously to meet a given situation.

The idea is to bring forth and support the richness of our being. In order to reclaim our identity as creative, responsive, compassionate human beings, we need to look, reach, and explore deep inside ourselves. We need to uncover the aspects of our being that lend brilliance, humor, and spontaneity to the situation. Our interest and curiosity are nurtured by our capacity to sustain "not-knowing." We can respond from a spirited, instinctual place rather than succumb to the oppressive, culturally-determined responses that applaud winning and being safe as the hallmarks of humanity. If we make winning and being safe our goals, we are destined to fail. When our lives are organized around aggression and defensiveness, then domination, control, and approval become the motivating factors for our actions. How can we support the outrageous, wild, and tender parts of ourselves if we are focused on winning and being safe?

By researching ourselves with the spirit of inquiry, we can discover our richness, our pain, and the truth of our pain. As we strengthen our hearts and bellies, we can learn to accept and make space for our pleasure and our pain. The ground of our being is our capacity to tolerate all that life brings. Our capacity for breath and feelings creates the size of our container. Are we willing to hold life in its fullness, just as it is, each moment fresh and new, arising out of the mystery? It takes tremendous courage, but it is "do-able."

Another aspect that has been emerging for me is the grandmother, the wise one, the ancient spirit within. My grandmother sits inside my womb, at the center of my *hara*. She brings me the gift of stillness as she sits wrapped in a blanket, completely still. When I remember to bring my attention to my belly, I can sense my grandmother's presence, there inside my center. For a brief moment, a second or two, I can feel, be with, and connect to this aspect of stillness. This does not necessarily mean that I become still. I may be feeling frightened, angry, or restless while I am aware of a stillness in my being. I am still angry and yet there is stillness. If I can rotate or shift my attention back and forth, I do not feel so completely identified with my anger. I am more aware that it is energy that is arising within me. Yes, the energy is there. And, so is the stillness. I am alive, teeming with responses on cellular, electrical, and emotional levels. Anger and stillness can coexist. The elements of life are not excluded from each other; they can enrich each other.

Exploring these aspects of ourselves is only one way of working with our richness. Taoists use the qualities of the natural elements to gain insight about how we interact with life—earth, air, fire, water, wood, and metal are primary teachers. We can explore parts of ourselves that are fiery, watery, or earthy. If we look to nature and open ourselves to her as our teacher, she offers a multitude of lessons about the attributes of the elements. By looking at how these elements interact with each other, we can learn to feel and recognize how these same qualities interact inside ourselves. Perhaps, we can see how we drown our fires of inspiration with the water of our fear because we are afraid of burning too brightly, or how we fan our fires of desire with the wind of gossip or ghosts from the past. We can recognize how our water can change, making us feel murky and soggy or clear, bubbling, and fluid. We can contact the deep oceanic feeling of patience and power within ourselves.

With so much potential for life within us, why do we limit ourselves so? Why do we choke and starve our innate curiosity and vitality with our desire to be "right" or "safe?" The intuitive part of ourselves is always there, ready to offer its wisdom if we are willing to make the effort of an archeological dig to uncover it. When we do dig into ourselves, sometimes a wondrous cavern opens fairly easily, while at other times, we have to really work and use great effort to dig down through many layers. Along the way, we may find some artifacts that give us clues as to how we previously lived or tell us of the destructive forces that crushed or wiped out an innocent, pure part of ourselves. Everything beneath our surface is our rich legacy. We have experienced birth, famine, death, and rebirth inside ourselves. An ancient knowledge within us understands these cycles. We have the capacity to love, be wounded, and love again. We can know, not know, and know again. We can move back and forth from warrior, adult, grandparent, and child as water, fire, wind, or earth interact inside of us.

Chapter Fourteen

The Path Never Ends

Remember, YOU are "expressing" the technique and not "doing" the technique ... like sound and echo without any deliberation. It is as though I call you, you answer me or when I throw something to you, you catch it, that's all.

Your task is to simply complete the other half of the "oneness" spontaneously. There is nothing to "try" to do. In the final stage ... techniques are all forgotten. Everything simply "flows."

Bruce Lee

In March of 1992, I injured my knee fooling around with a student during a private aikido lesson. For many weeks, I was barely able to walk and the recovery process was, and continues to be, extremely slow. Actually, I injured my knee twice.

The first time I injured my knee, I tore some cartilage and ligaments but not terribly badly. I used every waking moment and many methods to heal my knee—bodywork, visualizations, salves, and massage. I was obsessed in my efforts because my favorite teacher was arriving to teach a seminar in two weeks and I was quite fixated on training during that seminar. My knee improved swiftly although it was far from healed when my teacher arrived. My ego attachment to training and having him throw me overrode my sensibility. While training with my teacher during the seminar, I re-injured my knee. This second time, my knee was injured very badly—this injury stopped me.

In retrospect, I see that the universe had been tapping me gently, saying, "slow down." I had been investigating vulnerability and not-knowing in the conscious embodiment classes. I discovered that I needed to stop "doing" and start "being" more. I was aware of this message but my habit of "doing" clouded my perception. My desire for approval and control was a seductive enticement to train during this seminar even with a severely injured knee. By training, I thought I would be "better," I would be approved of, and then I would be in control. Ah, the mind obsessed with desire and attachment is a worthy opponent indeed. The second injury was a message so loud and strong that I had to hear it: "Stop. Stop doing. Stop even trying to heal yourself. Stop efforting altogether. Just be. Be here. Be injured. Be open. And, be vulnerable."

My ego was aghast. Fear flared. My identity felt shaky. If I am not able to roll and fall, spin and jump around, then who am I? I continued to teach, but my movement was so limited that my teaching style and technique had to change completely. Before the injury, I taught by having people throw me and then giving them feedback through my body. Now I could not fall at all; I could only throw. And even the throwing had to be done very, very carefully. I remember coming to the edge of the mat to begin class. The students would be lined up, in *seiza,* waiting for the "bow in." I would look down the line and think, "Why are they here?" I felt altogether inadequate.

After awhile, I found that the small, subtle details with which I had to work because of my limited movement, were fascinating to all of us. The micro-world of aikido has plenty to offer if we can stop, slow down, and explore areas where contact is made. My feelings of inadequacy began to be mixed with amazement and appreciation. I began finding new parts of myself based on what I could not do.

The process of healing this knee injury was completely different than my previous experience. The first part was to heed the strong message: "Do not heal it. Just be injured and vulnerable." After awhile, I slowly began to encourage healing. As I started working with visualization, an amazing and powerful experience occurred inside of me. I had been in the habit of calling on O Sensei's energy and presence to help me restore order in my knee. But during this time, when I was intending O Sensei's spirit to enter into my knee, I had a sudden visual and sensate impression. I saw a chapel, with a rose window, that appeared in the very center of my knee. My view was from the back of the chapel and there was a female figure very like the Virgin Mary in the front pew. She was completely still and praying silently.

I had this visual experience many times but I could never see her face because I was always at the back of the chapel. The message was "DO NOT ENTER: this is a sacred space being held in stillness by the feminine." No "doing" energy was allowed in to heal or fix my knee. What I found uncanny was that the chapel was always there. When my knee was doing well, the light from the rose window would be really bright and when my knee was stressed, the light was dim. As my knee improved with time, the size of the chapel began to shrink, allowing healing to occur slowly around it. This process lasted for about six months. As my spirit began to surrender and integrate my body's limitations and my knee began to gain more stability, the image of the chapel eventually dissolved.

Strangely, despite all of my concentration on my knee, I do not remember the exact time when the chapel was no longer there. One day, I realized that it had disappeared, vanished, and I could focus my intention into the inner structure of my knee. I could imagine the meniscus knitting itself together, the ligaments and tendons reattaching and tightening back up, the blood flowing through the area bringing new life to all of the cells.

Like so many transitions in our inner life, this change happened without my realizing it. The appearance and disappearance of the chapel was as if the Universe was the ultimate illusionist executing a sleight-of-hand trick. Where did the rabbit come from? Where did that umbrella disappear to? Rather than dissect the situation with the scalpel of the rational mind, which may very well be an illusion in itself, I chose to let my heart feel the sacred space within myself.

There are times to stop trying to fix or transform things, and be still while allowing ourselves to be held by the stillness. At other times, we are called to action—to build, to encourage inspiration and inquiry. Sometimes, what seems to be a misfortune is a blessing in disguise. My knee injury helped me to find aspects of my softness and my femininity that had not been able to emerge because my go-getter warrior was so dominant.

One of my favorite stories, a well-known Buddhist story, illustrates this point:

> There was a farmer who had a beautiful horse that he loved very much. One day the horse ran away.
> "What a terrible misfortune," said his friends.
> "We will see," replied the farmer.
> A few days later the horse returned with another horse.
> "Oh, how lucky you are," said his neighbors.
> "We will see," said the farmer.
> A few days later the farmer's only son was thrown from the horse, breaking his leg and crippling him for life.
> "Oh how terrible, what a pity," said his friends.
> "We'll see," said the farmer.
> A few days later some soldiers came through the town taking every able-bodied young man to war. . . .

And so the story goes on and on. In all our lives, many things happen over which we have no control. Even so, we are essentially free. We are free to choose whether we will echo the voice of the friends and neighbors, or adopt the perspective of the farmer. . . .

The Dance of Clarity and Obscurity

For all of us who are attempting to find our way along our path without the help of a specific external guru, there are many unsure moments. We may feel like we are hacking our way through a jungle, half guessing and half sensing the true path. Sometimes we feel like we are wandering in the desert. The possibilities seem so endless and we are desperate for a sign that we are on the right path.

Not long ago I drove up to Mount Shasta for a visit. I could see this venerable mountain more than 150 miles away, its special golden glow rising above the flatlands of the central California valley. For the next two hours the peak was a beacon of the landscape, rising above everything else. Even Mount Lassen, another grand peak, was diminished by Mount Shasta. The mountain was like a magnet drawing me toward it. As I entered the foothills and began my ascent into the mountains, an interesting thing happened—Mount Shasta disappeared.

As I wove my way through the canyons and along the side of cliffs, I could not see any sign of the gilded peak. Intellectually I knew, because I had been there before and I had also looked at a map, that the mountain was indeed ahead of me. But my body, wanting the visceral quality of energetic connection, was bewildered and anxious. I found myself straining around each corner, hoping to get a glimpse of the peak again.

At last I rounded a curve and there was the mountain, larger than ever, dazzling in its snowcapped brilliance. A sense of relief, confirmation, and excitement flooded my body, while my mind was saying, "How silly, of course it was there the whole time." From anywhere in the town of Shasta, where I was staying the night, I could see the mountain rising sharply into the sky. The next morning I decided to drive up the mountain and pay my respects to its great beauty and special energy. As I was driving up the side of the mountain, I again lost sight of the peak completely. Then, near the place where the road ends, the vista opened and the peak presented itself in all of its glory.

As I took my communion with nature there on the mountain, I realized that the sequence of clarity and obscurity I had experienced—being able to see the mountain and not being able to see it—was the same kind of experience that happens on a spiritual path. There are feelings of elation and confirmation when the view is clear, and feelings of anxiety and confusion when the view is obscured. What struck me was the necessity of keeping on, of not giving up even when we cannot see our goal.

This willingness to go forward is the quality of *irimi*, the willingness to enter into what is unknown. We must be willing to "hang in" and not give up our practices when things are difficult. When we look at a spiritual path from a distance, it seems so clear and so attractive. Perhaps we think that we too will be relaxed, loving, free from conflict. We jump on the train and begin the practices, imagining that nothing but good can happen. But after awhile we run into ourselves, our fear and aggression, and the mountaintop is obscured from view. The training of *irimi* can help us to continue. If we center, become stable and soft, and then move forward, we will reach a place where, for awhile, things again become clear.

Our Human Prerogative

> I said to the almond tree,
> "Sister, speak to me of God"
> And the almond tree blossomed.
>
> —St. Francis of Assisi

How can we encourage ourselves to be explorers investigating the vast possibilities and intricacies of life? Most of our phenomenal capacity for humanness is taken for granted. We cut ourselves off from ourselves as we try to shore ourselves up with supplies of knowledge, judgment, and criticism to defend ourselves against our "enemies"—growth, change, and death. By learning about and educating ourselves as to who we are, our darkness and our lightness, we can begin to become whole.

As Thomas Merton said, "What can we gain by sailing to the moon if we are not able to cross the abyss that separates us from ourselves?" If we can connect to ourselves, then we can make genuine connections to others. Our relationship to ourselves is reflected in our relationship with others. As our anxiety and hostility toward ourselves is softened, our defenses can begin to come down. We can begin to dismantle the fence, the barricade which surrounds us. We are intrinsically connected to all things in a mysterious way. When we lose sight of this connection, we lose one of the greatest ethical and behavioral reference points of our humanness. "Am I my brother's keeper?" Maybe. But, surely, I am my own keeper. If I can keep myself healthy and whole, and if all things are connected, then without any extra effort I am naturally, through my own way of being, having a similar effect on all things. We must tend to the whole situation of our lives.

Our compost pile needs to be turned over. And at the right time, this rich mixture of broken dreams, pain, and fear and the fermented wisdom of our past seasons is spread upon the ground to enrich the soil and nourish our new crop of insights, ideas, and visions. Birth, growth, change, fruition, death, decay, and rebirth lead to more growth in a continuous, ongoing cycle. All of this happens naturally, whether we like it or not. It is our choice, our human prerogative, to open to life, to appreciate it, be awed by it ... or not. The choice is ours.

The mountain peak is there, whether we see it or not.

Part V

Practice Guides

The following outlines are quick guides for practicing the techniques discussed in this book.

Utilizing Your Breath

This is introduced and discussed in Chapter Two, pages 23–24, and demonstrated on the videotape The Intuitive Body.

- Direct the exhale downward in a clockwise direction towards the *hara* point, or the center of the earth; think of the exhale as moving in the same direction as closing a jar.

- Make the exhale audible.

- Sustain your exhale as long as possible.

- Focus on the inhale.

- Bring the inhale up from the earth in a counterclockwise direction; think of the inhale as moving in the same direction as opening a jar.

- Feel your breath moving through your body and the sensations that arise.

In spiral breathing, the inhale draws up from the earth through the body in a counterclockwise direction and the exhale flows down through the body into the earth in a clockwise direction.

Each of us has an energy field or energetic presence that surrounds our bodies and communicates some sort of message to others and our environment. The message may be "come here," "go away," or something else.

Balance is important in our energy field as well as in our bodies. For a feeling of more balance we can ask the question: "Is the front of my field equal to the back?"

Balancing Your Energy Field

Explained in more detail in Chapter Two, pages 24–25, and demonstrated on the videotape The Intuitive Body.

ASK: Is the front of my field equal to the back?

Is the left of my field equal to the right?

Is the energy above my head equal to the energy below my feet?

PAUSE: Feel the sensations that arise.

Sense any reorganization of your energy field.

Feeling Gravity

Explained in more detail in Chapter Two, page 25 and demonstrated on the videotape The Intuitive Body.

• Be interested in the pressure of gravity on your body.

• Feel the weight of your body.

ASK: Can I feel the weight in my feet? (if standing)

Can I feel the weight of my arms? (if standing or sitting)

Can I feel the weight in my buttocks? (if sitting)

PAUSE: Feel the sensations that arise.

Evoking and Choosing a Quality

Explained in more detail in Chapter Three, pages 33–34, and demonstrated on the videotape The Intuitive Body.

- Choose a quality you already possess yet want to develop.

- Have your quality be something you have felt before and want to feel more of.

- Select a word that represents what you want to become, for example: gentle, kind, compassionate, intimate, vital ... and make it a quality, such as gentleness, kindness, compassion, intimacy, vitality....

- **Avoid** choosing a quality based on a **should.**

ASK: If there were more (*the quality*) in my being, what would that feel like?

- Focus on the place between asking the question and when the response occurs.

- Wait for a sensation to arise.

- Do not attach great importance to the response.

- Ask this question more than once.

- If no sensation surfaces, try another quality or word.

Basic Practice

Explained in detail in Chapter Two and Chapter Three, and demonstrated on the videotape The Intuitive Body.

Basic practice combines the previous exercises for breath, balance of field, gravity, and quality. See the outlines above for more detail. As you become familiar with these exercises, you may want to use this abbreviated form:

Breath:

- Bring your attention to your breath.
- Exhale, spiraling downward, clockwise.
- Inhale, spiraling upwards, counterclockwise.
- Feel the sensations that arise.

Balance:

- Check the perimeter of your field for equal distance from center to front, back, right, left, above, and below.
- Feel the sensations that arise.

Gravity:

- Be interested in the pressure of gravity on your body.

ASK: Can I feel the weight of my body?

- Feel the sensations that arise.

Quality:

ASK: If there were more (*the quality*) in my being, what would that feel like?

- Focus on the place between asking and when the response occurs.
- Feel the sensations that arise.

Spiral-Breath Meditation

Explained in more detail in Chapter Four, pages 40–41.

- Begin by sitting or standing comfortably and closing your eyes.

- Imagine that the bottoms of your feet are open and that the energy of the earth can be received through them.

- The inhale moves in a counterclockwise direction, up from the earth, and is associated with cleansing or purifying.

- The exhale moves in a clockwise direction, down from heaven, and is associated with strengthening or empowering.

- Use these nine areas of your body to focus your breath:
  Draw the breath in through the bottom of your feet into your ...
  Ankles ... then to your
  Knees ... then to the
  Pelvic floor and genital area ... then to your
  Hara, or belly, ... then to your
  Solar plexus ... then to your
  Heart ... then to your
  Neck ... then to the
  Center of your head, behind your eyes ... then
  Draw the breath through the top of your head as it spirals out toward heaven.

- Take one to five breaths in each area, depending on the health or strength of that area.

- When you lose concentration in any area, start on that area again or do extra breaths to bring your awareness back into focus.

- Having moved your breath through your whole body, relax and allow your breath to flow naturally.

- Retain an awareness of the purifying inhale moving counterclockwise and the strengthening exhale moving clockwise.

- Pause as if you are about to hear, feel or see something: the not-knowing state.

- Feel the sensations that arise.

- When the time for ending arrives, reorient to your breath, inhale spiraling up, cleansing, and exhale spiraling down, strengthening.

- Check the perimeter of your field in all directions.

- Shift your attention to sensations of heaviness or lightness.

- Evoke your quality.

- Open your eyes and move around, allowing the experience of the meditation to stay with you.

In spiral breathing, the inhale draws up from the earth through the body in a counterclockwise direction and the exhale flows down through the body into the earth in a clockwise direction.

"Yes, ... And, ..." Technique

Explained in more detail in Chapter Five, pages 48–49.

Whenever the negative, critical internal voice arises, go with it for a moment and make the blend using this technique:

> *"Yes,* that is true. *And,* if there were more *(the quality)* in my being, what would that feel like?"

- Pause and feel any sensations that arise.

- A new perspective on the situation may come with the sensations.

Any kind of judgment, negative or positive , is a distraction from the direct experience. By using the "Yes, ... And, ..." technique, we can shift our attention from our judgments to the experience of the moment.

Positive/Receptive

Explained in more detail in Chapter Nine, pages 84–85, and demonstrated on the videotape The Intuitive Body.

- Practice walking backward and forward.
- Switch off, first walking backward and then forward.
- Keep switching until both directions begin to feel the same.
- Test yourself with a partner.
- Can you keep your awareness of the front and back of your field when you are in relationship with someone else?
- If it is difficult to keep your field balanced when in relationship to someone else, this is fine because you have something to work towards.

Dropped Attention

Explained in more detail in Chapter Ten, pages 87–89.

- Dropped attention is the starting place for focusing attention.
- Focus just on yourself.
- Bring your focus within yourself.
- Create some attractive inner images of yourself, perhaps with colors, scenes, sounds, textures, or anything else that stimulates pleasant associations.
- Allow yourself to be with yourself.
- You are alone—it is just you and you.

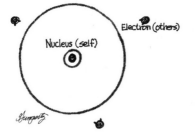

When we are in "dropped attention," our attention is focused on our own energy field and bodily sensations. We are not distracted by others because we are so interested in our field and connected to our body.

With "contracted attention," we may move both physically and energetically away from others instead of toward ourselves. This kind of contraction is directed by an obsession with the other instead of centering on ourselves. We are off center and not balanced when our attention is contracted away from others.

With "ellipted attention," we get so involved with the other person that our sense of self is lost. We are off center and not balanced when our attention is ellipted onto someone else.

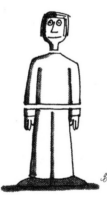

"Split attention" within ourselves frequently indicates an internal conflict. Splits can be at the solar plexus, separating the head and heart from the belly, or at the neck, separating the head from the heart and belly.

With "split attention" outside of ourselves, our awareness is separated from our physical body as though we are watching our experience from somewhere outside of ourselves.

Open Attention

Explained in more detail in Chapter Ten, pages 89–91.

- Open attention is moving from dropped attention to the state of "self and included others."

- Apply your imagination, perhaps in a "let's pretend" manner.

- Expand your energy field or attention in all directions—to the back, front, right, left, above, and below.

- Imagine you are the nucleus of an atom and the people around you are the electrons.

- Stabilize or hold the space for those inside your field.

ASK: How deep do I need to be? How wide do I need to be to hold the space for those inside my field?

- Keep sensing the width and depth of your field.

- Allow movement to take place without grasping or resisting. *Remember: you are stabilizing the space or environment, NOT trying to change the people in it.*

- Accept others completely and make space for their entire range of behavior—this is the Buddhist sense of compassion.

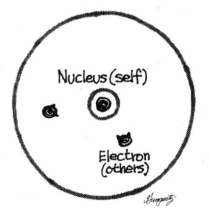

When we are in "open attention," our attention is expanded as we hold the space for ourselves and for others. Using the metaphor of an atom, we can imagine that we are the nucleus responsible for stabilizing the space for others who represent the electrons.

Metta Meditation

Explained in more detail in Chapter Three, pages 31–32.

- This is a three-level practice.
- Begin with making requests for yourself.
- Make the same requests for loved ones.
- Expand to make the request for all sentient beings.
- End with repeating the request for yourself.
- Requests may be: "May I be happy. May I be peaceful. May I be filled with love." *Or, when asking for others:* "May they be happy. May they be peaceful. May they be filled with love."

For information regarding *The Intuitive Body* videotape, workshops, and seminars, please contact:

Wendy Palmer
809 Vendola Drive
San Rafael, CA 94903